"BUT CAN SHE TYPE?"

Janet L. Kobobel
Overcoming Stereotypes in the Workplace

INTERVARSITY PRESS
DOWNERS GROVE, ILLINOIS 60515

InterVarsity Press is the book-publishing division of Inter-Varsity Christian Fellowship, a student movement active on campus at hundreds of universities, colleges and schools of nursing. For information about local and regional activities, write IVCF, 6400 Schroeder Rd., P.O. Box 7895, Madison, WI 53707-7895.

Distributed in Canada through InterVarsity Press, 860 Denison St., Unit 3, Markham, Ontario L3R 4H1, Canada.

All Scripture quotations are from the Holy Bible, New International Version. Copyright © 1973, 1978, International Bible Society. Used by permission of Zondervan Bible Publishers.

Cover illustration: Roberta Polfus

Diagrams on pp. 54-55 by Jane Wrede

ISBN 0-87784-513-1

Printed in the United States of America

Library of Congress Cataloging in Publication Data

Kobobel, Janet L., 1948-
   "But can she type?"

   Bibliography: p.
   1. Women in the professions.   2. Women executives.
I. Title.
HD6054.K62   1986   658.4'09'024042   86-21001
ISBN 0-87784-513-1

17	16	15	14	13	12	11	10	9	8	7	6	5	4	3	2	1
99	98	97	96	95	94	93	92	91	90	89	88	87	86			

To Judy,
who taught me more
than either of us
ever realized

People's names in the undocumented
examples have been changed
so each person is unidentifiable.
The women who told me their stories
wanted anonymity, and most
of the men would, I'm sure, vote for
the same if they had the opportunity.

Preface

Some unwritten law deems it imperative that an author explain just why he or she wrote a certain book. All I can say is that I frequently lament to God: "Why couldn't I have written a book on *29 Ways to Stay Awake During a Sermon* or *How to Complete an Afghan in Just Fifteen Years*"? As far back as colonial days, men were appointed to roam the church aisles, tickling dozing parishioners' noses with feathers. And ever since crafts became a hobby, people have broken records for the longest delay in completion of a project. These subjects stand firm in the solid soil of time-worn topics.

But, no, here I am, writing a book on the shifting sands of women's roles. As new patterns swirl with the desert winds, the setting and our responses to it keep changing. Responses in 1976 simply won't do in 1986. And, in 1976, no one would have dared to even think about what's actually being lived out in 1986.

But that's the point. That's why books *need* to be written. We're all busy exploring and making new discoveries about the nature of women and how to express that nature in society. We need to share our discoveries to learn and encourage one another.

That's what this book is. An internal exploration given external expression. What started out as intense, private struggles with my womanliness evolved into a decision to write it all down. Then, what started out as a description of my odyssey turned into a four-year project that included one year wearing out a library chair as I researched sociological and psychological studies. What started out as opinions became convictions. I share my findings with you today, knowing that tomorrow there will be more discoveries that will require new books. Maybe you'll write one of them. Then you'll understand how vulnerable I feel as I push this manuscript in my publisher's direction.

As I hand it over for publication, my mind turns to special people who made special contributions: Gary, Alan, Kathy and Randy, who read the manuscript—or endured having it read to them. Rather than sticking out their tongues, they offered kudos.

Sybil, who understands that books cost more than a sane person should pay.

Roy, who through word and deed helped me find my many selves.

All those who prayed and supported when my zeal flagged, especially Jean Pankey. When no one else seemed to remember to pray, she did. When it seemed everyone else thought of the book as a sidelight in my life, she let me know she knew better.

Gail and Joy, who typed the book and stuffed me with chocolate chip cookies.

The women who openly told me about their struggles to be womanly—and godly—leaders.

Everyone who had the courage to ask, "How's the book?" knowing they would receive groans and sighs in reply.

PART 1

The Working Woman in a Man's World

CHAPTER 1

The Door of Opportunity

The opportunities for women are expanding so quickly, it's enough to destroy you."[1] With this simple lament, one woman expresses the plight of most women today—opportunities yawn deliciously yet cavernously before us.

Women in leadership positions have become an inevitable reality of life for better or for worse. And the trend continues. "Today's businesswoman is part of the expeditionary forces moving into the executive suite," career consultant Lawrence Schwimmer stated in *U.S. News & World Report.* "Within 19 to 20 years, we'll begin to see women in presidential, CEO-type positions."[2]

Some women seek long and fight hard for leadership positions. A few drift upward in their organizations with no special plotting or planning. However a woman scales the heights—through choice or mere circumstance—once in a leadership position, she makes one quick but haunting observation: "I'm alone."

Just Me

She is the only woman in the meetings, at the luncheons, in the conferences, with a chair with armrests. She has few or no female predecessors in leadership. She may well be the first woman in her organization to hold her position.

And even in the moments she manages to forget she is a woman among the men, the men inevitably say or do something to snap her back to reality. Especially at first, questions incessantly present themselves:

How does my womanliness merge with my job?

How should I respond to the men when they single me out as the woman?

What do I do with the inevitable fact that God created me a woman?

With few models and probably few female peers, she must forge for herself an appropriate expression of who she is in that position. At this point, many of us opt for the most obvious choice: emulate our predecessor, usually a male. "Womanly" thoughts are ignored and discarded as invalid. Words like "assertive" or "logical" come to be prized when applied to us, especially when they emanate from the lips of male coworkers.

We can't help wondering if the more powerful positions open to us will destroy us as women. Even as we sense great potential loss, we also know the possibilities and promise of greater leadership. The tension comes in seeking some elusive balance. It's a tough post for a woman to hold—to be a leader and to be a woman—and few have done it successfully. It can be done. But it takes all the mettle one can muster, combined with the conviction that even women should have the freedom to excel in the workplace . . . shouldn't we? Or is this view closer to the truth:

A businessman is dynamic; a businesswoman is aggressive.

A business man is good on details; she is picky.

He loses his temper; she is crabby.

He's a go-getter; she is pushy.

When he's depressed, everyone tiptoes past his office; When she is moody, it must be her time of the month.

He follows through; she doesn't know when to quit.

He's confident; she is stuck-up.

He stands firm; she's hard as nails.

He has the courage of his convictions; she is stubborn.

He is a man of the world; she's been around. . . .

He isn't afraid to say what he thinks; she's mouthy.

He's human; she's emotional.

He exercises authority diligently; she is power-mad.

He is close-mouthed; she is secretive.

He can make quick decisions; she's impulsive.

He's a stern taskmaster; she's hard to work for.[3]

That little ditty jests about how a chauvinist differentiates between two career-centered people. But, as in most humor, it purposely distorts a truth. Both men and women harbor doubts that a woman can gracefully hold her own in a leadership position. And even more important, many believe she should never have tried. She should have stayed home, where she belongs.

No Competent Women

Even women avoid reporting to other women and tend to consider them less capable than men. A study conducted among college women asked them to read various professional articles. One group would read an article with a man listed as the author. Another group would read the same article with a woman's by-line. The students consistently attributed greater impor-

tance to the articles supposedly written by the men. They saw
the men as more authoritative not only in professions usually
considered male but also in neutral and even female professions, such as nursing. They harbored a clear bias against wom-
en as competent people.[4]

Further bad news comes in several studies in which individuals compared the qualities of a good manager with the qualities inherent in men and women. In one such sampling, men
and women rated ninety-two descriptive terms, stating which
ones they believed applied to men, which to women, and which
to managers.[5]

The following list shows the qualities they believed were most
frequently true of both men and managers:

emotionally stable
steady
analytical ability
logical
consistent
well-informed

The next list reveals the qualities the group most frequently *did
not* associate with women:

emotionally stable
steady
analytical ability
logical
consistent
well-informed

Such results are heart-rending. But they only objectify what a
woman in leadership already knows. The moment inevitably
arrives when all the warning signals flash within her—she is
being dealt with not as a person but as a woman—a woman
who is out of her element.

I remember well my first "but you're a woman" encounter.
Fortunately, nothing quite like it has happened since. I sat at

my desk on a hot summer day, explaining to John, a man several years older than I, that he had just breached policy and would need to redo some work. After this pronouncement, I viewed a kaleidoscope of manipulative responses.

First, John portrayed the little boy who is sure Mommy isn't serious and will change her mind if he pouts. When I remained staunch in my decision, he played the strong man who willingly relieves the woman of her overpowering burden. Seeing that role fail, his brown eyes seemed to darken. This time he attempted to beseige my right to make decisions, playing the part of the man who is forced to deal with the incompetent woman.

As John rushed through these several approaches, all in a matter of minutes, I explained over and over that I was willing to adjust my decision if he could logically express to me why I should.

But apparently John was not able to deal logically with a woman. He seemed sure that only appeals to my emotional nature would succeed. Finally, he left my office stymied because his strategy had not worked. As I watched him walk out of the building, I felt strangled by frustration and found myself responding as childishly as he had. I hoped he would hit his head on the window air conditioner that had leveled several preoccupied people in the past. But he didn't. So, I rallied my mental energy and thought about why I was so frustrated.

Asking a coworker to redo a project is hard enough. But because John and I couldn't view each other as persons, the situation had become several times harder. We were prisoners in our male and female compartments.

A Woman Is . . .

That little incident set my mind racing. Should women leaders be treated differently from men who lead? Are they different? If they fully express their womanliness as leaders, how do they do so? If they stifle their womanliness, are they leading as capably as they could? Or is stifling their femininity the only way to be a competent leader? How do I bring glory to God as I express myself in my work environment?

These questions and further opportunities to watch men like John in the working world eventually led me to write this book. I want to explore with you, first, the conflicts we experience in our careers, why we experience them, and how we can deal with them. Then, we will consider whether men and women are different and what that means to us in shaping and honing workable leadership styles.

CHAPTER 2

Inner Conflicts

While *men and women may* stand together in their conviction that a woman shouldn't lead, the woman in leadership stands alone against her internal struggles. A woman who aspires to lead must overcome some complex inner conflicts: the decision to pursue a career vs. the pull of marriage and family; and the fear of leaving a secure position for one that offers challenge and risk. She channels vast energy into dealing with these and other conflicts.

Career vs. Marriage: Tension #1
One of the foundational frays a woman enters is whether she wants a career. Surprisingly, it takes her a long time to even realize she must answer that question.

Early in life boys reckon that they will have to work to support themselves. But most girls are taught to find someone to support them. As I grew up, my father looked with skepticism at expenditures such as life insurance and college. After all, he pointed out, a husband should provide me with security of every kind. It seemed reasonable at the time. But I rather haphazardly ended up in college anyway.

After college, I launched into my career as most women do, by taking a job. That's all it is to a woman at that point—a job. It's a place to bide her time until she fulfills the traditional role of getting married and having a baby. One friend described this attitude as "circling the airport." The woman has no sense of direction: she is simply waiting for the moment when she can land on the spot marked *marriage.*

She carefully chooses not to appear too interested in her job. What if a young man ambles by as she intensely pores over the papers on her desk? She's battling with the question, if she realizes it or not, Can a woman be a fanatic about her profession and still be marriageable? Most women answer no. One researcher responded to the query this way: "Yes she can [remain marriageable], for I know some, but I think a woman must be abnormally bright to combine charm with concentration. These women make the synthesis by being charmingly enthusiastic."[1]

A serious career tends to increase certain qualities in a woman—independence, decisiveness, assertiveness—which are generally not deemed ideal in a wife.

But studies show these attributes are a part of many women's personalities even before they take responsible positions. It's woven into the fabric; the only question is what form it will take. In reality, the strong woman probably would have trouble living out a traditional role even if she *did* decide to circle the airport.

What should a woman with a propensity to lead do? "Be all you can be," my supervisor wisely advised me when I was a few years out of college. "Be as strong as you can be and trust God to bring a man into your life who is strong enough to comfortably and intimately relate to you." Later God did just that for her. She lived out her own advice, and God gave her a husband who appreciated her strength and encouraged it.

It hasn't worked out so neatly for me, and sometimes I grumble to God—and cry—about the injustices of a society that seems to find a woman intimidating because she's capable. But I keep coming back to a point of logic: I can't find anywhere in Scripture that God tells me to hold back, to stick my abilities in my hope chest, to practice batting my eyelashes. I enjoy my career. As I once told a fellow, "I *love* to bake bread—on my day off."

A Question of Talents
One day, to help myself regain God's perspective on my gifts, I rewrote the parable of the talents, incorporating a modern setting and contemporary characters. The new version went like this:

May 15
Dear Diary:
Today Mr. Drake called Craig, Carol and me into his office. We all bustled in, carrying the prerequisite yellow pads, the insignia of junior executives. We sat in a semicircle in front of his mahogany desk like a fine autumn scene in hues of gray, brown and navy—all dressed for business success.

He explained that he needs to be gone for the whole summer on a business trip. The responsibility of keeping the company functioning well rests on our shoulders.

He gave the prize departments to Craig to oversee, of course. It's obvious he's priming Craig to replace him when he retires. Carol was given a couple of departments of medium importance with some sticky problems. I'm glad I was spared those! But me, I got the department no one cares anything about—and just one department. What a blow; I feel like a popped balloon. How can I prove I'm a capable, competent leader with so little to work with? I've lost out again!

Sept 3
Diary, dear one:
I've had a heartbreaking day at work. Mr. Drake reviewed Craig, Carol and me on our summer performances. Craig got a whopper of a promotion because he solved some major problems in his areas.

"Such creative insights," Mr. Drake said while he patted Craig on the back. "You deserve the vice-presidency. Come on over to the house tonight to celebrate."

Then he flipped through Carol's reports as if he couldn't believe the good news. "Carol, double the production—in just three months! How about a raise and a couple more departments to manage? And you come over tonight, too. How about 7?"

As he turned to me, a cloud replaced the balmy atmosphere in the room. "Joyce, what happened? It's as if you were invisible. Production and profits haven't wavered one iota from the beginning of the summer. The summer is our best season!"

What could I say? I couldn't think of anything.

"Joyce, I believed in you. I knew you could come through the summer with fanfare. I had a promotion in mind for you that would have suited you perfectly."

I untied my tongue when I saw his concern. "Mr. Drake, I just couldn't seem to stir up myself to take any action. I wanted to succeed, but I guess I didn't want it enough to overcome my inertia." By this time I was crying.

But Mr. Drake didn't hand me his handkerchief or anything. He looked at me until the strength of his gaze forced me to look at him. "Joyce, because of your incompetence, I'm going to have to demote you and let Craig see what he can do with that department."

What?! How could that be!! I knew Mr. Drake could be a tough man, but surely this wasn't happening!!

But it's true; I'm back to an entry-level position!

I'm devastated. I can't sleep; I can't eat; I'm a wreck. I want my job back!

My little version of the parable of the talents certainly isn't inspired, but it reminds me that my God has every right to *take away* any responsibilities or gifts he has given me if I'm slovenly. I might be careless out of fear, or because of an unclear focus on where to concentrate my energies, or because of half-heartedness. But he has every right to call me on the carpet if I don't use my abilities. I suspect he would rather have me wholeheartedly risk much and lose all in an attempt to grow than hold myself in reserve until I become a wife.

How could I ever explain to God that I held back developing myself while I moved through my twenties and into my thirties in *hopes* of finding a husband? I don't think he'd be any more impressed than Mr. Drake was with Joyce. It is with this perspective that I strive to achieve in my career. Not to look good for others but to be everything I can be for God, to develop the talents he placed in me from the beginning.

But if a woman refuses to circle the airport and develops her talents instead, then conflict may arise when she does marry. Research conducted on perceptions of the ideal woman shows that both men and women believe she should nurture her family *and* develop herself. Generally, men responded positively to the woman's being active outside the home.

But when it came to rating specific statements about marriage and children in women's lives, the men often contradicted their general opinions. In other words, the men at first said they endorsed women's involvement in outside pursuits. But when specific application was tested (for example, should a wife work, go to school, be active socially), the men reneged. They really wanted the woman to stay at home.[2] Women also were uncertain in their views of women's roles, probably reflecting the contradictory cues they received from men.[3]

And so society continues to waffle between encouraging and discouraging women to take their jobs seriously. Meanwhile, women opt for a lukewarm response to the jobs they have, withholding a major portion of themselves as they nebulously plan on a more traditional female role a bit farther down the road.

Moving On Up: Tension #2

Most women don't grapple outright with the marriage-career tension, especially in their early twenties. Nor in their twenties do they tend to reach a clear-cut decision to vigorously pursue a career. They simply acquire the postgraduate job. Some of them decide to be competent in that position, but they give little thought to the future.

If the woman remains in that position until her early thirties, she'll probably discover that her job has turned into a career. Not by choice, but by happenstance. Unfortunately, about the time she makes that discovery and begins to think about advancement, she realizes that she has not developed the skills to advance. She has treated her job as a job—a detailed task to be learned well and performed reliably. But she has not looked for new opportunities or ways to expand her skills. Doing so now demands especially high risk and change because her job has become part of her identity.[4] Failure would be much more difficult to handle at this point.

A man, in contrast, enters his first job with the notion he'll advance out of it as quickly as he can. He reaches a middle management posture far sooner and more economically than the typical woman. And, on the way up, he makes certain he learns from each new position what is necessary and valuable for the next. On each rung of the ladder, he gains broader experience and understanding of how the organization functions.

Like the woman, he learns a technical skill. But, unlike the woman, his investment in that skill is not particularly deep. She has to make an in-depth investment to create a positive impression and gain security in her own eyes and the eyes of others. His security rests in his potential, *not* in a technical skill.[5]

At the transition point, the woman fears being cut off from an area she has mastered in depth. Since her sense of legitimacy and security emanate from the familiar, it's tough to confront new and different problems, new and different people, in a setting where she may be the only woman.

While the woman is consumed by conflict and internal fears at this point, the man's concerns center on the people around him: Can he surround himself with peers who can use their expertise to help him? Will he find capable subordinates? Will his boss be a man he can learn from?[6]

Meanwhile the woman retreats within herself. She becomes afraid to ask questions because maybe she should know the answers. She works on her own time to learn the job's details. At that point, the apparent confidence of the men around her only makes her feel more isolated and insecure.

Carolyn is a typical example of a woman who walked backward into a career. Before she became the assistant director of surgery for a large Denver hospital, Carolyn fussed over details like any well-trained nurse.

"I excelled in my practice as a technician," she says. "So I was made a manager of people. I felt *very* unprepared. As a nursing student, I had been trained to take care of patients. No one ever prepared me to take care of employees. And I was the youngest nurse in the department."

Armed with one prime principle her parents had taught her—the Golden Rule—Carolyn set out to manage twenty-four operating rooms and one hundred forty employees.

"Four years after I took the position and after lots of management training, I finally *really* got a handle on the functions of the job," Carolyn confesses. "Then I realized the emphasis of managing wasn't functions but people."

It took Carolyn four years to fully grasp how she should manage her area because she was unprepared psychologically and professionally for the position.

Who, Me?

I, too, strongly identify with the typical career-woman path. I received my first supervisory position amidst protests from only one person—me. Since I wasn't in a career mode and enjoyed what I was doing before, I didn't see any reason to take this new position. Plus I didn't think I could effectively supervise.

Being prone to hyperbole, I pictured myself in my new job ramming wild-eyed through the halls, slamming subordinates against the walls if they didn't get out of my way. (All this from someone who is 5′ 3″!) *I* wouldn't want to report to the aggressive, overbearing person I knew I became whenever I was under pressure—and the supervisory position was a high-pressured one.

But the job was bestowed on me, and surprise of surprises, I soon learned to love it. I discovered I had a career *and* many of the personality qualities that work well in leadership (including the ability to care intensely for the people who worked for me). I wasn't wild-eyed after all.

But I did have an eagle-eye management philosophy, watching all the jots and tittles of my area. Since I was now in charge of quality control for all the company's printed material, the job enhanced my pickiness.

Thankfully, a more skilled manager taught me the basics of

delegating. That's why I survived. But several years later I switched to teaching communications in a seminary.

Alone

I moved from a position of authority over a building full of people to being an instructor with no one reporting to me. I moved to being the only woman faculty member in an assertive and articulate group of men. Also, most of my students were men, some older than I. I was intimidated.

"Hide in your ofice," all my instincts shouted. But I was committed to succeeding because I had become committed to my career. Along the way I had decided not to knit my life around a future family. I wanted to utilize all the abilities God had granted me in the situation he had placed me in. To do less, to circle the airport, was to deny that I was an individual gifted by God *so that* I could give to others. Even today my mind understands and adheres to that idea, but my heart strays and needs to be called back to the business at hand—which is my career, not marriage.

Like me, most women grapple with at least two types of internal conflicts: Will they choose to pursue a career or simply have a job and hope for a family? Will they develop their abilities or stash them in their hope chest?

Some Personal Helps

To help you establish where you are in your career attitudes, complete the following exercises:

1. Tailor-make a passage of Scripture to a career issue you struggle with (use the remake of the talents parable earlier in the chapter as a pattern). As you write, retain the passage's meaning but adjust it to your specific situation. Ask God for spiritual eyes so you can see the situation as he wants you to. Ask him for spiritual ears so you can hear what he has for you in the situation. Ask him to apply that specific Scripture passage

to your circumstance.

Here are some suggested passages if you are unsure where to begin: Matthew 6:25-34; Matthew 18:23-34; Matthew 20:1-16; Mark 10:35-45; Mark 12:41-44; Luke 15:11-32; Luke 18:9-14.

2. Put an X on each line to indicate where you think you are:

Circling the airport	Setting my sights on new job challenges

Hiding my talents in my hope chest	Developing myself without fear of becoming intimidating

Stuck on developing a technical skill	Busy broadening my experience

Afraid to advance	Willing to advance if given the opportunity

Look over your Xs and then write a prayer in response to their locations. Ask God to show you what attitudes need to change and to give you the wisdom to know how and the courage to do so.

CHAPTER 3

The
Only
Woman

Bonnie, *the director of the chil-*
dren's ministry in a midsized southern California church, sat
down with the new senior pastor. Pleased to have the chance
to get to know him better, she eagerly leaned forward in her
chair. After a few preliminary remarks, the pastor admitted,
"Bonnie, I have only one thing against you—you're a woman."

Kathy, a church staff member for one and one-half years, was
perplexed as she sat on the sanctuary's platform. As she surveyed the overflowing Easter congregation, she wondered what
she was doing on the platform. She had no part in the program.
She had never before been asked to sit on the platform with
the other staff members. But the senior pastor had asked her
to today. "Why?" she wondered. Was it because it was Easter?
Did the pastor want to make a statement about a woman's place

in the church? Had he suddenly realized she wasn't included in the church staff "group" up front? Whatever the reason, being up there just didn't feel right.

Both women face a common conflict for women in leadership—that sense of being an "other" or a "token." The word *token* doesn't necessarily mean that Kathy was on her church's platform just for show, or that Bonnie was chosen because the church wanted a woman in its structure. It does mean that Kathy and Bonnie were the only ones of their kind (women) in their environments. Rosabeth Moss Kanter was the first person to use *token* to refer specifically to women in the work environment. The term is now used by many authors in this specialized way.

Kanter observed that even having a few of a minority group creates a token situation. A ratio of 85:15 makes the 15 tokens. Because of the small number in the minority group, they tend to be seen as representative of that whole group: symbols rather than individuals.

That's how tokenism works: A set of objects will be seen in a certain way based on the number of different types of objects in that set. If there are nine boxes and one circle, the circle

stands out. Some won't even see it, but if it is seen, it will get more notice than any box. At that point, the boxes tend to look pretty much alike—because they all look different from the circle. Generalizations are made about circles because only one is visible. (All circles are a certain weight; all circles are a certain height; all circles have rims of a certain thickness.) Not as many generalizations are made about boxes because different types can be seen. The same perceptual factors come into play when a woman works in a predominantly male environment. That position generates pressures and conflict for the token person.

Kanter identifies three important stresses for women in corporations.[1]

In the Limelight

First, women face the difficulty of receiving extra attention simply because they are women. Kanter found that "everyone knew about the women. They were the subject of conversation, questioning, gossip, and careful scrutiny." One woman, on a business trip to Atlanta, swore in an elevator in the presence of her colleagues. A few days later, back in the home office in Chicago, everyone had heard the story and had labeled her a radical.[2]

Living in the limelight places pressure on the woman not only to perform well to advance her career but also to represent all women. As Kanter states,

> Some women were told outright that their performances could affect the prospects of other women in the company. In the men's informal conversations, women were often measured by two yardsticks: how *as women* they carried out the sales or management roles; and how *as managers* they lived up to images of womanhood.[3]

So a certain sense of responsibility for all women is placed on the one woman.

I sometimes made decisions to be involved in aspects of the seminary where I taught because I didn't want the men to think that women shouldn't take part. I wasn't particularly interested in the activity, but I knew I was setting expectations and standards among the men for what women should and should not do in the future.

Receiving attention isn't all bad, of course, because if you succeed, everyone notices. But, as one woman said, "If it seems good to be noticed, wait until you make your first mistake."[4]

Sticking Out

The second conflict a token woman experiences is that of contrast. The dominant members of a group become aware of all the things they have in common with one another while they observe their differences from the minority. That exaggerates the differences. Men may ask if it's okay to curse or discuss sports while a woman is present. Or they may fuss over whether they should open doors for her.

I felt out of place at our school's faculty meetings. Because we were a Christian school, prayer was an integral part of our gatherings. The person who opened in prayer usually asked God to make us "men of God." Fellow faculty would address our august group with, "Men, we need to . . ." or "Men, don't you think . . ." I wondered if I were invisible.

Members of the dominant group don't always acknowledge the presence of a token. But if they do, they usually ask her feelings in front of the whole group. Does she mind if they talk football? Would she like them to open the door for her? If she says it's not okay to discuss sports or that she would appreciate having doors held for her, she's telling them that she is indeed different. They are not free to act as they would like to do.

If she tells them to, in essence, pretend she isn't there or that she isn't different, then she is denying her own identity and trying to fit in at all costs. Plus, it *isn't* all right for her to talk sports or open a door for a male colleague. If she asks to be treated "special" or to be ignored, she becomes an observer to conversations.

Being Stereotyped

In addition to receiving special attention and being contrasted to men, there's a third pressure for women—blending. The token is seen as fitting into the stereotypes of her group. She is not given the freedom to be an individual; she is Woman personified.

For example, a woman in an unusual job setting is assumed to be in a typically female role.[5] When someone knocked on my office door looking for another faculty member, he or she would often assume I was a secretary.

Sometimes blending occurs when certain positions within an organization are thought of as "the woman's slot." In other words, once a woman has occupied a certain position, that job is thought of as a woman's.[6] If the director of a certain department is a woman, when she vacates that position, management is more likely to think about replacing her with a woman.

Bank tellers are a good example of this. A job once held by men, it is now commonly thought of as a woman's job—and the position is not viewed with the respect it once was.

Finally, women can lose their identities as male coworkers blend them into roles they are familiar with; for example, the mother or the kid sister.[7] Peers aren't necessarily choosing to stereotype women; they just don't know how to deal with someone who doesn't fit into any assigned boxes. A man may think, "If I can't talk sports with her, what do we talk about? But if I think of her as my kid sister, that helps."

People subtly force the woman into a category so that they know how to relate to her. The woman can comply with these expectations and play the role or decide to be herself. It's a lot like moving into a new community. People try to "place" you via questions and observation. The overt questions are designed to classify you:

"Where do you work?" ("How can I place you according to education level and interests?") "Where do you live?" ("How can I peg you according to income and lifestyle?")

At work, much of the same process unfolds. It pays to be aware of what's really being asked so one does not end up labeled and cast into a box. How you answer, "What did you do this weekend?" *can* make a difference. Being yourself is probably the best safeguard against being cast in a role. But sometimes it doesn't matter what your response; only time will enable your coworkers to see you as uniquely you.

Of Male and Female Schlemiels

All of these things may not happen to any one token. Nor do they happen only to tokens. Any newly hired person could feel pressured to perform, uncertain about acceptance, and either overprotected or abandoned. But these stresses *do* tend to happen to tokens more consistently than to others.

Every time there is a new position, new peers or a career transition, a woman will probably find herself a token again. Women are still scarce in many settings. And women, for some time, will need to work harder and expend more energy than the average man to succeed.

As the president of a corporate search firm said, "Equality is not when a female Einstein gets promoted to assistant professor. Equality is when a female schlemiel moves as far as a male schlemiel."[8]

The good news (and there is some) about tokenism is that it forces a woman to master herself in a tough situation. That builds character, perseverance and self-esteem. The bad news is that the situation drains off a great deal of psychological energy.

Several biblical characters found themselves experiencing the good news/bad news of being a token. These people were in foreign environments, feeling the heat of the limelight and wishing they weren't so "other."

Esther hid her difference (her Hebrew lineage) until it became imperative for her to tell her husband-king that she was Jewish. Because a decree had just been proclaimed that Jews were to be killed, for Esther to speak up and say she was part of that minority was to lay her life on the line. But she did, displaying graciousness and wisdom in how she handled the delicate situation, and saving her people.

Hosea was appointed by God to be a token of sorts by marrying Gomer the harlot—not exactly a popular practice in any society. He gave his children names which would remind Israel of God's response to their unfaithfulness. Thus his children also became tokens who stood out in social situations. Imagine calling your children, who are playing outside, at dinner time: "Not Pitied, Not My People, Scattered—time for dinner!" At that moment, you, the children and the neighbors would all remember your token status.

Daniel and his three Judean companions were trainees to serve in their captor's palace. Their nationality singled them out as did their insistence on eating a vegetarian diet rather than the goodies from the court-appointed training table.

Each of these people suffered the distresses of being different to a far greater degree than any woman leader I know. But each came forth with sterling character as he or she chose to grapple with tokenism rather than rush pell-mell out of the situation.

Plan A or Plan B

Besides running, the typical woman seems to have two realistic choices.[9] First, she can accept isolation and be the audience. Her peer relationships will remain friendly but distant, and she may be excluded from informal social gatherings where important decisions are made.

Or, second, she can try to become an insider. The price for that decision is losing her identity and disassociating herself from other women. That, in and of itself, is a pressure.

When I was faced with these choices I tried to find a middle ground. After a year of remaining the Silent One at faculty meetings and listening to us "men" being addressed, I decided to take action. After talking over the options with my roommate, I headed toward the vice-president's office and asked for a ten-minute slot in our first fall faculty meeting.

I tackled the issue of inclusive language by talking about the terms the apostle Paul used to refer to groups of people. None of those terms, I pointed out, were sexually differentiating. Yet at our school we had chosen to deviate from this time-honored pattern. So I suggested some silly alternatives to replace the offensive word *men* in faculty meetings. Some of the terms were based on school abbreviations and slang; others on regional preferences since we had faculty from all over the U.S. and from Britain.

My ridiculous suggestions fortunately succeeded in pointing out the problem without making people defensive. Humor won out.

I learned some important lessons that day that can help out in other sticky situations. The most important is that women should act rather than just react. Sometimes we think our role, especially when we're in token situations, is to accept and respond to others' actions. We forget that we can take initiative and bring about change. The hardest part may be mustering up the courage to act; sometimes making others aware of a need is all that's required.

I also saw that assuming good of others is a healthy place to start in most instances. If we're careful *not* to assume that there is deliberate prejudice or ill will—if we give people the benefit of the doubt—we may find that our colleagues are genuinely surprised to hear that they have been offensive. Don't assume that it's *us* versus *them*.

Using humor is important. We all accept messages much more readily if they're conveyed with warmth and good will. When I first began to plan my presentation, I was serious and lethal. My roommate had the foresight to strongly advocate a funny presentation. I suspect if I'd given my original now-hear-this message, I would have found few sympathetic listeners.

Tokens can tend to take themselves too seriously. Margaret Mead describes being a token as like being a foreigner:

As the member of another culture fumbles and stumbles in a different land, with hand stretched out for a door knob that isn't there, a foot raised for a step that is missing, an appetite that rises insistently at an hour when there is no food, and an ear trained to wake to sounds that are never heard in these strange streets, so the immigrant coming into an occupation that has been the sole preserve of the other sex will stumble and fumble and do less than is in him or her to do.[10] Fortunately, one does adjust to a new culture. But it takes time.

Making It Personal

1. Read one of the narratives of a biblical "token" that we've briefly discussed. Esther—the book of Esther, chapters 1—8; Daniel—the book of Daniel, chapter 1; Hosea—the book of Hosea, chapter 1.

What correlations do you see between the pressures that person experienced and those you are experiencing?

What decisions did he or she make before God?

What action did he or she take?

How can you translate those decisions and actions into your situation?

2. Draw a circle, representing the personal interactions of your coworkers. Let Xs represent the people you work with. Show significant relationships by the placement of Xs in or outside the circle. Then put in an O representing yourself and your relationship to your peers. The O may be outside the circle, on the rim, clustered with a group of X's, etc.

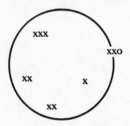

If your circle shows you're experiencing the conflicts of a token, decide how you'll respond:

☐ I'll wait for the storm to blow over in a couple of years and meanwhile accept isolation.

☐ I'll try to become part of the group by differentiating myself from other women and being "one of the guys."

☐ I'll look for a creative way to let others know I'm aware of the situation and help them to relate to me comfortably.

I plan to implement my choice by _____

(plan of attack)

_____ .

The first person I plan to begin with is _____ .

I will do so by _____ .

(date)

CHAPTER 4

Do We Fear Success?

Complete *the following story:* "After first-term finals, (Anne, John) finds (herself, himself) at the top of (her, his) medical-school class . . . "

That projective test, given to college students by Matina Horner in 1968, became the foundation for the theory that women fear success.[1] Women who completed the story wrote endings such as this:

Anne (female subjects wrote about Anne; male subjects wrote about John) starts proclaiming her surprise and joy. Her fellow classmates are so disgusted with her behavior that they jump on her in a body and beat her. She is maimed for life.

The males' stories tended to have happy and satisfying conclusions:

John is a conscientious young man who worked hard. He is

pleased with himself. John has always wanted to go into medicine and is very dedicated. . . . John continues working hard and eventually graduates at the top of his class.

Horner concluded that the women's negative views fell into three categories: social-rejection fears; worries about womanhood; and denial of reality.

Social rejection fears:
Anne is an acne-faced bookworm. She runs to the bulletin board and finds she's at the top. As usual she smarts off. A chorus of groans is the rest of the class's reply.

Worries about womanhood:
Unfortunately Anne no longer feels so certain that she really wants to be a doctor. She is worried about herself and wonders if perhaps she isn't normal. . . . Anne decides not to continue with her medical work but to take courses that have a deeper personal meaning to her.

Denial of reality:
Anne is a code name of a nonexistent person created by a group of medical students. They take turns writing exams for Anne.

Horner found that sixty-five per cent of the women, as compared to ten per cent of the men, wrote stories that fell into these three categories. She concluded that success contained bittersweet elements for women because it raised the conflict between achievement and femininity. It also implied that aggressiveness, which is presumably inappropriate for women, had been employed to succeed.

Chiefly based on Horner's dissertation, which received wide publicity after a summary of it appeared in *Psychology Today,* the phrase *fear of success* became associated with women. Men and women seemed to agree that a strong argument for not advancing women in organizations was that women weren't sincerely interested anyway. Hence fear of success looms as another conflict for the woman who wants to lead.

Each of us could probably offer stories of how others have communicated their belief that we don't want to achieve. One day, as I tried to explain to my supervisor that I was inundated with work and that we needed to institute some long-range solutions, he responded by saying: "If your home life were happier, you'd feel better. Why don't you find some new roommates, or better yet, aren't you dating anyone?" His motives, I think, were good. In his mind, if I were more content with my personal life, my job wouldn't be so important to me. Then I wouldn't care about succeeding. In his mind, that would make me like other women.

The Other Side of the Coin

But a number of studies since Horner's, although receiving less publicity, question the validity of her testing and all the assumptions that have grown from it, including my supervisor's. One researcher found that women aren't anxious about achievement per se, but about achievement in areas that violate sex-role norms.[2] To support the belief that it was fear of cultural violation rather than actual fear of success that stimulated the answers to Horner's story, the same story, using first Anne and then John, was given to men and women. *Both* sexes gave more negative responses to Anne than to John. But the men showed more negative responses to Anne than the women did.[3]

One author suggests that fear of success is actually fear of visibility, stemming from the token concept. She saw Horner's test as measuring pressures for women to keep their achievement invisible and to deny success. She pointed to a test that showed that for many years Jews at Yale responded as women do today. At that time, Jews were tokens at Yale.[4]

Rosabeth Moss Kanter also saw an alternative explanation: depressed aspirations. "There is much evidence that people have low aspirations when they think their chances for mobility are low."[5] She went on to explore two sociological studies that brought an ironic twist to the popular picture of women as intrinsically less committed to work than men. One study showed that work is *not* a "central life interest" of factory workers by using a sample of men. The second demonstrated that work *is* a central life interest of professionals by studying an all-woman sample of nurses—women who did have opportunity.[6]

In the first study, men with low opportunity to advance looked like the stereotype of women at work: they limit their aspirations, seek satisfaction in activities outside of work, dream of escape, interrupt their careers, emphasize leisure and consumption, and create sociable peer groups in which interpersonal relationships take precedence over work.

Peer networks, Kanter proclaims, become supremely important to those who believe they aren't upwardly mobile. In one firm she studied she found that

as a woman rose in Indsco, she was likely to find fewer female peers, whereas men found a male peer group at every level of the system. So concern about "leaving friends" and the social discomforts of a promotion were often expressed by women in clerical ranks; men in management had no such problem. One secretary said to another who had recently been promoted, "*I* don't want to get promoted. Then I'd have to eat with the men."[7]

The key to understanding this antisuccess attitude, Kanter states, lies in recognizing that two statements are intricately tangled together: "I don't want to _____" (achieve, advance, move) and "I can't _____" (achieve, advance, move).

As one woman on a church staff said, "I do what I'm allowed

to do and don't fret about what I can't. I just look the other way when, as a woman, I'm refused an opportunity."

Kanter's sour-grapes arguments seem sound and worth considering. But there's another, equally plausible explanation for the variance of interest in success between men and women.

What Is Success?
Other researchers conclude that success, as defined by men, is not of prime importance to women, but successfully combining career and relationships is important. In 1981, Matina Horner herself said: "Now, with career women more accepted than in the '60s, the fears are more often related to guilt over the impact of a career on personal relationships."[8] In other words, in a woman's dictionary, *success* has a different definition.

Successful men seem not to harbor concerns about career vs. relationships. Jane Adams, in her book on successful men, reports asking them to weigh the components of happiness. Recognition, professional success and financial accomplishment counted far more heavily than such factors as being in love, friendship and social life, spouse's or partner's happiness, personal growth, physical attractiveness and sex life. One man said, "Success doesn't make a man happy; it *is* happiness."[9]

Adams states that women view balance in life as an asset; to successful men, it's a "distraction and a disadvantage."[10] Men are willing to be gung ho about one element in life, whereas women define success in terms of balance. If a woman has one without the other, she will judge the single "success" as hollow, a mere echo of what she really desires in life. Recent tests show that women who *do* manage to juggle marriage, family and career have a stronger sense of competence and a richer view of themselves.[11]

One test of young women showed that they desired to combine home and career but despaired of being able to do so. The women were grouped into "creatives" and "controls" based on personality characteristics. The researcher reports that a previous test showed that

> on the threshold of adult life before career and marriage choices are made, there is little difference in the important personality traits between men and women. Yet [in comparing the women] four-fifths of the creative women as compared with one-third of the non-creative controls reported having experienced overwhelming feelings of emptiness, desolation, and aloneness. Preoccupation with thoughts of death and even suicide were common in the creative group.[12]

The researcher offered two possible explanations for the despondency: it reflects greater emotional intensity in the creative women than in the controls; or it reflects the potential these women feel they have and the despair in believing they will have to choose between their femininity and their intellectual capacity.[13]

Counselor Esther Matthews believes, based on her experience, that the latter discouragement is the greatest. She calls this "the shadow of self." She sees gifted girls and women constantly torn between wanting and needing marriage and wanting and needing to use their gifts and abilities. The woman is never sure which portion of herself to thrust into the light and which into the shadows.[14]

In motivation tests, men are found to be strongly motivated by needs for achievement and sexual gratification; women have a need for emotional support from others, love and security.[15] When the need for strong relationship shows up in a talented woman, she often forges her own definition of success.

As successful women were surveyed by Jane Adams for her book *Women on Top,* she found that many of them didn't aspire to the very top positions in their firms, even if they thought they could get them. Adams concluded:

> Achieving women are not afraid to be different from other women, or to be seen as somehow less than feminine; their

real problem turns on issues of independence and balance. As one woman aptly put it, "I'm not afraid of success because it makes me substandard as a woman. . . . I'm afraid of success because it makes me too much like a man. And that's a very important difference."[16]
For that woman, to be like a man meant to harbor a false sense of success. She would have none of it. And that's true for many women today. It isn't that they fear success; it's that they refuse to succumb to the easy but destructive view of success that has dominated the business scene.

Matina Horner says: "Young people today, who are seeking a more balanced life, are questioning the either/or choice [family vs. career]—and that is good. It is a mistake to get all one's reward out of any one kettle of fish."[17]

Burgeoning Barns

Not only is this view of success more complete, it's also more in keeping with the Bible's portrayal of achievement. Let's first look at what the Bible says success is not.

The fellow who built bigger barns (Luke 12:13-21) to contain his burgeoning (agricultural) success, miscalculated in one way: God was using a different arithmetic. God's math added up success not in barns but in love—loving God and your neighbor with every corpuscle of your being. Not that you can't have a big barn and love at the same time, but concentrating on a fine, broad barn and its content is an emphasis that gets you an embarrassing title: fool.

Daniel presents a study in success according to God's math, a success that incorporates love of God, neighbor and self. Daniel pressed to achieve but pleased God in how he did it. Look over the following checklist to see if you're as dedicated to a balanced success as Daniel was. Would you:

1. Aim to be the most knowledgeable and the wisest among your peers (Daniel 1:17)? _____ yes _____ no _____ maybe

2. Dare to distinguish yourself by asking to do the unpopular thing that you were convinced was right (1:11-14)? ____ yes ____ no ____ maybe

3. Be cool enough in a crisis to use brains and tact rather than emotional appeals (2:1-15)? ____ yes ____ no ____ maybe

4. Take aggressive action when circumstances squeezed you like a toothpaste tube (2:16)? ____ yes ____ no ____ maybe

5. Base your aggressive action on the belief that God would undertake for you and pray with others that he would (2:17-18)? ____ yes ____ no ____ maybe

6. Praise God when he does rescue you (2:19-23)? ____ yes ____ no ____ maybe

7. Make sure your supervisor knows God deserves the credit (2:27-28)? ____ yes ____ no ____ maybe

8. Remember your friends when you succeed and advance them if possible (2:48-49)? ____ yes ____ no ____ maybe

9. Refuse to allow material rewards or career advances to be your primary motive (5:13-17)? ____ yes ____ no ____ maybe

10. Be so trustworthy, conscientious and uncorrupt that your enemies have to institute new, immoral regulations to place a banana peel in your path (6:3-5)? ____ yes ____ no ____ maybe

11. Refuse to live according to those immoral regulations, regardless of what price you have to pay (6:10-11)? ____ yes ____ no ____ maybe

12. Know that regardless of what successes or failures the future holds, you are firmly held in God's hand (12:9-13)? ____ yes ____ no ____ maybe

Obviously, in God's book, success emanates from much more than a focus on collecting positions, power and prestige. Character and care for others figure in big ways.

Setting a New Trend

Women can do themselves *and* men a favor by helping us all bring more balance into our lives: to work hard at our jobs without sacrificing close relationships and service to others. But severe difficulties can arise when the woman's two major roles conflict and a choice must be made between them. Such conflicts *will* arise. So the question becomes, How will the woman and those close to her deal with conflict when it comes? Hennig and Jardim suggest that if a woman consistently communicates that her career is an integral part of her life, then when crisis intrudes the family can respond as a unit.[18]

They cite an interview they conducted with the only woman in a sales group of twenty-nine men. She had won her company's yearly award for highest individual sales. The winner from the year before congratulated her and gave her the name of the person who had framed his certificate. She said, "Can I come into your office and look at it?"

He replied, "Well, it isn't there. It's hanging in the family room at home. I'll bring it in."

She thought, "What's wrong with him; why isn't it in his office? He won it for what he does here. Mine is going to stay here."[19] Hennig and Jardim pursued the topic:

We asked her if she could . . . describe [her husband's] understanding of what it was she did at work. She found this extremely difficult to do. . . . We asked her how she managed if for instance their son were ill. She said that of course she missed work. . . . We asked if she could really afford to miss work on a day when she was to meet with a really important client. . . . She guessed she could ask her husband to stay. Would he? She'd have to persuade him. What would that involve? She threw up her hands. "I guess I'd have to start right at the beginning and tell him what my job was about, why I had to go and why he had to stay." Would he be more easily persuaded if he were already aware of what her job involved and what it meant to her? She said, very slowly and very thoughtfully, "I think I'll take the award certificate home."[20]

That decision was, of course, a display of her serious intent to be a success—at home and at work.

On to Success

What if you find yourself stymied at work by others' assumptions that you like your corner of the world and want to remain in it? You can . . .

1. Look for your supervisor's pet peeves and volunteer to help solve problems associated with them. Or volunteer to do research that would help your supervisor solve them. Just make sure that if you do the research, people on your supervisor's level are aware of it so you get proper credit.

2. Volunteer for high-visibility projects, such as those that are especially important or rushed, or those that cross several departmental lines. But first be fairly sure you can do well; don't get in over your head!

3. Tell your supervisor in what ways you would like to further develop your career. (Don't tell your supervisor your goal is to get his or her job!)

4. Take night classes that relate to your job and bring suggestions to work based on what you've learned.

5. Call to your supervisor's attention articles or books you have read that deal with a problem he or she is trying to solve or a new area the company is thinking about developing.

6. Ask your supervisor for critiques on work you have done, communicating a willingness to grow and learn.

7. Be willing to put in extra hours to complete a big project.

8. Write memos offering solutions to some office bugaboo. For example, suggest the mailboxes be moved out of the supervisor's secretary's office into a more central location so the secretary isn't interrupted so often. Or that your supervisor ask

Mike to plan the office parties since he is the office social butterfly but has a head for details and is creative.

9. If you're married and travel is an important route to advancing, announce you *can* travel. It's usually assumed a married woman would rather not, especially if she's a mother.

Past Traditions

One element that might help us twentieth-century women as we attempt to break with traditional thought is an even earlier tradition: The models of women of the past. In the Middle Ages in Europe women handled all of the spinning industry, dyeing industry, weaving industry, catering industry, the brewing and distilling industry, the preserving, pickling and bottling industry, the bacon curing, and a large share of the management of landed estates since the men were gone for months at a time on war and business.[21]

Tax registers from that era show women frequently involved in occupations: doctors, apothecaries, plasterers, dyers, scriveners, miniaturists, bookbinders. Women were so autonomous during the Middle Ages that they weren't even expected to take on their husbands' names. That practice began in the seventeenth century.[22]

Ironically, women began to lose many of their freedoms in the Renaissance. During that "golden age" Roman law was reintroduced to consolidate political power and move it away from the fiefdoms. This same Roman law lowered women's status. Cardinal Richelieu saw women as an important political element to "de-power." "Nothing is more capable of damaging the body politic than this sex," he said.[23]

Dorothy Sayers points out the repercussions for removing the Medieval woman's responsibilities:

It is all very well to say that woman's place is the home—but modern civilisation has taken all these pleasant and profitable activities out of the home, where the women looked after them, and handed them over to big industry, to be directed and organised by men at the head of large factories. . . .

What is more, the home has so shrunk to the size of a small flat that—even if we restrict woman's job to the bearing and rearing of families—there is no room for her to do even that. It is useless to urge the modern woman to have twelve children, like her grandmother. Where is she to put them when she has got them? . . . It is perfectly idiotic to take away women's traditional occupations and then complain because she looks for new ones.[24]

So even though fear of success seems like a simple explanation for women's hesitancy to leap to the forefront in pursuing a career, too many other explanations are more plausible. The most likely is that women simply refuse to buy into the present view of success. And that's good. We need to continue to forge a balanced definition, to insist on a success that doesn't break down relationships or relegate them to the back of the bus. We must continue to search for a way to reconcile career, marriage, children and friends without sacrificing the quality of our work or relationships. It's a healthier approach than the business world has endorsed in the past, and it's a view with a history of its own.

Personalizing

1. To help you better understand your view of success, picture yourself as a white-haired woman, blowing out the candles on your eightieth birthday cake.

a. What do you want people to acknowledge you for achieving in your lifetime?

b. As the people at your party turn to one another, what do you want them to say about you?

c. What gives you satisfaction and inner peace as you try to huff out your candles?

d. Now . . . ask God if you need to make any midcourse corrections so you *can* experience that satisfying eightieth birthday party. And check out with him if your goals are the ones he has in mind for you.

What plans do you need to add? Abandon? Adapt?

What could you strive for in the next five years to move you in that direction?

What internal hindrances do you see to your plans?

What fears?

What tradition-bound thought patterns?

What restricting view of yourself?

What can you do to begin to overcome these hindrances?

2. To gain perspective on what is worth pursuing and why:

a. Go to a retirement home and ask several residents two questions:

What is the most important thing you've achieved in your life and why?

What was your greatest failure?

b. Read the book *Miriam* by Lois Henderson (Harper & Row) and study Miriam's fluctuating motivations. What were the results in her life and the life of others as she struggled with her reasons for wanting success? Make a list of positives and negatives for each motivation as you complete each chapter of *Miriam*.

Motivation: _____

	Positives	Negatives
Effect on Miriam		
Effect on others		

CHAPTER 5

Male and Female Differences

Female and male . . . *is one* from birth innately assigned pink bows and the other blue bow ties? Is one a dusting of sweet seasonings and the other an earthy combination of snails and playful pup? Or are they of the same ilk? As a woman struggles to figure out who she is in relation to her business peers, she wonders: "Am I really different because I'm a woman?"

One concept that has gained popularity in recent years proclaims the answer is "No, not really." Called androgyny, this belief states that "it is both possible and desirable . . . for *both* males and females to possess *both* what are traditionally known as masculine virtues and feminine virtues."[1] You don't hear it labeled by its official name too often, but it saturates the media. John Naisbitt, author of *Megatrends,* thinks androgyny is the eleventh American megatrend.[2]

Masculinity and femininity have been viewed in a variety of ways throughout the history of psychology.[3] Some have purported that masculinity and femininity are two distinct boxes, with rigid sides to each box (see Fig. 1). A person must fit in his or her appropriate bit of cardboard to be accepted and to be considered healthy.

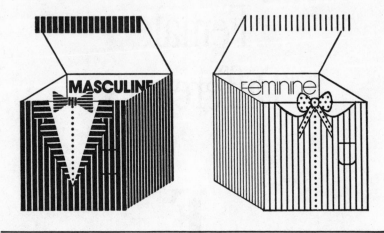

Figure 1

More recently, masculinity and femininity have moved out of the boxes and onto a continuum (see Fig. 2). Some people are considered very masculine, some moderately so, some moderately feminine, some very feminine. With masculinity and femininity at opposite ends of the pole, they are presented as opposite qualities.

◀MASCULINE▮▮▮▮▮▮▮▮▮▮▮▮▮▮▮▮▮▮▮ Feminine▶

Figure 2

But androgyny, which grew out of the ideas of Carl Jung, rejects boxes and continuums. It proclaims that a person can be very high in femininity and very high in masculinity at the

Figure 3

same time (see Fig. 3).

The androgynous person is presented as the woman who plays tennis well, enjoys wearing jeans, is committed to her career, but loves to make her own pasta and wear a stunningly feminine outfit to the theater. Or the man who is always up for a strenuous hike, but along the way finds a wild rose and sits down to write a poem about it.

Best of Both

On the surface androgyny sounds fine—a melding of the best

of both worlds. And certainly it is a healthy trend for men to express sensitivity and for women to be more assertive. But androgyny takes a good concept and overdoes it. Like deciding purple is your favorite color and decorating your house in un-relenting shades of it.

Androgyny has inherent problems. It presents an ideal that may not be real. It requires each person to be the renaissance person, capable in a multitude of areas, expressing equal gifts in crafts, arts, sports and relationships while being a connois-seur in everything from teas (loose leaf, of course) to literature. This new cultural tyranny asks each person to be a knotted combination of contradictions (forceful and dominant while shy and soft-spoken). And, ultimately, it demands that there be no difference between men and women. We must all strive to be the Ideal Neither.

Jan Morris (James Morris before the operation) wrote on androgyny in *Vanity Fair* and claimed that the sexes are becom-ing alike, "converging upon some physical medium." Morris predicted sex would die out in a couple of thousand years; perhaps, she pondered, "we are all on the road to intersex."[4]

Even though Morris is an extreme, she exemplifies androg-yny's greatest problem. Carried to its natural end, it results in a denial of the difference between the sexes. And there is a difference. Science finds it even exists in the structure of men's and women's brains. As one author said, "From the hypothal-amus, the center for sexual drive, to the cerebral cortex, the seat of thought, scientists have found consistent variations be-tween the sexes."[5]

Neuropsychologist Jerre Levy has done special research in studying the right and left sides of the brain and each side's unique work. The right side (hemisphere) of the brain tends to work with spatial relationships while the left focuses on lan-guage. Levy has found that brain-hemisphere dominance var-ies with gender, concluding that the right hemisphere dominates in the masculine brain and the left in the feminine brain.[6]

Levy also suggests that women's left and right hemispheres seem to share more tasks than men's. This could explain female intuition as well as male superiority in mechanics and math. The two closely connected hemispheres of the female brain would communicate more rapidly—an advantage in absorbing and sorting through all the facts and nuances in intricate situations.

But, Levy states, the connecting link is a disadvantage "when it comes to homing in on just a few relevant details." The man could utilize his right hemisphere more precisely in deciphering a map or locating a three-dimensional object in a two-dimensional representation.

Further Proofs

Other studies verify Levy's findings and make additional ones. Endocrinologist Anke Ehrhardt has discovered that some sexual behavior, such as girls' tomboyishness or boys' roughhousing, is influenced by hormones.[7] Other scientists suspect sex hormones control aggression and even fear.[8]

Rutger's psychoendocrinologist June Reinisch and UCLA's Melissa Hines independently studied children exposed before birth to a synthetic hormone to prevent miscarriage. Both found the hormone created more masculine traits in males and females. Hines concluded, "It is compelling evidence that prenatal hormones influence human behavior due to changes in brain organizations." Reinisch, who had thought that she would prove there was no effect, was taken aback by the strength of the evidence of her testings. She admitted that hormones "flavor" an individual for one kind of gender behavior or another. She added that culture certainly had its own strong seasoning to contribute to a person's intricate composition.[9]

Diane McGuinness studied the vast body of technical literature that has developed in this field. She concluded that from

infancy on, males and females respond in ways that provide
significant clues to their later differences in behavior. McGuinness believes the evidence is "compelling that sex differences
are a result of biological determinism."[10]

The compounded data lead to one clear conclusion—men
and women may make up one humanity, but even in such a
controlling and vital organ as the brain, they are different from
one another.

The Balance

That conclusion, however, does not force us back into a "box"
mentality as we view men and women, or to decide that it's
inappropriate for a man to be sensitive or for a woman to be
strong. Tests show that more creative men are more feminine
in sensitivity and intuition than less creative men. They also are
stronger, show greater confidence, determination, ambition
and power than other men.[11]

Other studies show that more intelligent and better educated
women score more masculine among women.[12] Androgyny
would seem to correspond with these tests, pointing toward a
greater wholeness, in which each sex's strengths would be advocated in the other. But the essential problem remains: androgyny ignores that there is a difference. Regarding the dangers
of androgyny, Anne Ulanov comments:

> We lose a clear definition of either [man or woman] to a
> blurry indefiniteness that masquerades as man-woman. That
> sort of identity differs significantly from the strong male who
> possesses large feminine sensibilities, or the vibrant female
> who manifests vigorous masculine qualities. The men and
> women who possess their contrasexual sides confidently and
> clearly stand out from the shapeless unisexual as flexible and
> open, large in their identities as men and women.[13]

So the problem isn't whether there is a difference: there is. The
problem isn't even a matter of degree—whether the difference

constitutes a mountain or a molehill. Instead it's what to *do* with that difference. We don't understand what the differentiation means.

Margaret Mead suggests that our present response to differences is shallow and untherapeutic: We attempt to obliterate or at least to minimize them.[14] We're quick to point fingers and utter words like "prejudice" whenever someone contends there are dissimilarities.

Mead's concern, which I echo, is that such a myopic view diminishes the possibility of complementarity in relationships. It mutes both male and female "to a duller version of human life, in which each is denied the fullness of humanity that each might have had."[15]

The woman who decides she will pursue a career struggles between expressing her femininity or being masculine or acting androgynous. One psychologist believes each career woman must go through a set process before she finds an identity that is comfortable for her and her colleagues.[16] Let's look now at that process.

Three Phases of Eve

When a woman first begins her career, she tends to strike a match beside her masculine qualities. She wants to light up that part of herself for everyone to notice, because it will gain her entrance into a masculine world. I call this phase the Masculine Masquerade. The woman is, in psychologist Esther Harding's word, "dogmatic" at this point in her life. She has an opinion about everything and is anxious to share it. She enjoys getting into arguments, not to learn but to convince.[17]

From this initial stage she moves on to the sophistication phase, which I call Occupied with the Occupation. She finds herself settled into her organization and working directly for what she wants. That is not usual for women because they traditionally must seek covertly to attain their desires. At this stage a woman becomes absorbed in a cause, which is an ideal to which she dedicates herself. (Harding encountered one woman who proclaimed she was working for the "progress of the universe," although when pressed, she really didn't know what that was.) In actuality, in this phase the woman has the masculine goals of striving for success and prestige.[18]

Some women go on then to the last phase, Harmony, in which the woman reconciles her masculine and feminine traits within herself.[19]

Even though they do not describe these phases, Hennig and Jardim found them lived out by the women they studied in *The Managerial Woman.*[20] They divided the women into two groups—twenty-five who made it to the top of their corporations, and twenty-five middle-managers who found themselves in dead-end positions.

Who, Me?

All fifty of the women began in the Masculine Masquerade phase. Phrases like "remain unnoticed as a woman," "be like one of the guys," and "never be accused of being like a woman" described this era for the women.

One woman expressed her view like this: "You fended off all attempts of men to treat you like a woman; you opened the doors before they could hold them, sat down before a chair could be held and threw on a coat before it could be held for you."

Shortly thereafter the women found themselves in phase two, Occupied with the Occupation. They became totally immersed in their careers. They clenched their teeth and determined to outdo the men. For these women, who entered their careers in the 1940s, it seemed the only way—outdo the men so you could match them step for step up the ladder.

They tended not to pursue relationships outside of work. And rather than calling attention to their femininity, they did their best to camouflage it. They based all relationships on the job to be done, ignoring any innuendoes, double meanings and barely disguised propositions. They didn't deny they were women; they simply avoided confronting what that meant because it might affect their ability to live out the goals they had set for themselves.

At this point, the women who remained in middle management came to a conclusion about the career-marriage issue: A woman needed to be a man at work and a woman at home. The other twenty-five women admitted they held a similar belief for the first ten years of their careers. Then, in their mid- to late thirties, they each hit a crisis point and realized they had to have greater congruence between their work and nonwork behaviors. This crisis was the entry point to the third phase, Harmony (so-named for the outcome, not for the process, which is an intensely painful one).

For the first ten career years, these twenty-five executive women had not consciously denied their sexual identity. They simply refused to engage it. As one woman said, at about age twenty-five she "had taken her femininity and stored it away for future consideration."

Then, as the Harmony phase began, a number of discoveries flowered in each of these twenty-five women: they developed a fresh security in their jobs; they began to relax at work; their careers lost much of their charm in terms of reward and challenge. And, as one woman said:

I began to realize that I was getting older and had very little in life other than that job. . . . I think, unconsciously at first, I was really concerned about being an unmarried woman reaching middle age too. I had always been able to avoid that one because I always saw myself as young with plenty of time to devote to that later—when I got the career under control. But there I was at thirty-five; time had crept up on me and I worried about things like not being able to have children

much longer. Life wasn't as exciting at work and life outside
of work was virtually non-existent.[21]

Social Butterflies

All twenty-five top women responded to this inner crisis in the
same way: They shifted their careers to the wings and pressed
their social and personal lives into the limelight. One called
herself a social butterfly during this phase while another admitted, "I felt like an adolescent again, starting out to achieve my
first date."

The women cast aside the severe colors and straight seams
of their wardrobes for softer colors and lines. They decided on
more clearly feminine hairdos and chose to look and act like
women. They concluded it was fine to look like traditional wom-
en because they wanted to be viewed as women—for the first
time in a long time.

They made a clear role choice, knowing that they would now
have to deal with the conflicts such a role selection would
cause. One woman described the conflict this way:

I was really petrified about going to work with this new look.
The first few days I got a lot of stares and double takes and
some kidding and whistles from people who knew me better.
Everyone seemed to look at me in a new way and so I did
at myself and I liked the way it felt to be looked at that
way. . . . I think that for once, I could distinguish that those
looks were specifically for me as a woman. I looked forward
to being noticed, to being admired by men that way. . . . In
that time I know that I changed forever. I learned to understand and accept, and yes, like and enjoy another very real
part of me.[22]

The women characterized the Harmony phase as the time they
became whole people, when they became mature women. They
came to grips with who they were. They now adopted a style
that challenged others' views of the traditional woman. There

they were, aiming at the top of their corporations, clearly and comfortably women.

They each reported relationships at work became freer and more open. They didn't feel the need to control and repress others—or themselves as women. They became free to let their own styles of leadership evolve. As they interacted with others, they were perceived as being more honest and real—and they were. As they recall this period, they describe themselves as "happy," where they used to use words such as "rewarded" or "satisfied."

They also dealt with the issues of marriage and family during the Harmony phase. Half of them got married to men at least ten years older than they, many to men with children. None of the women had children of her own. Those who didn't marry during this time remained open to the idea even in their fifties. Those who did marry considered themselves fortunate to have "unique" husbands who encouraged them to move ahead in their careers and avidly applauded each success.

All the women worked through these changes in two years or less and then returned to pursuing their careers with renewed vigor—and a new view of themselves.

Stuck

Meanwhile, the women in the middle-management group struck a different pose from the twenty-five who made it to the top. The major difference is that they never reached the Harmony stage. They never called a moratorium on their careers to settle the issue of their femininity. Instead, they remained faithful to self-concepts and behavioral styles that were predominantly masculine. They continued to believe that their sexual identity and their careers were in conflict, and they continued to suppress their femininity. They acted as though they were not women.

They evolved a bitterness toward the men "who stood in their way" and kept them from rising to higher positions. The majority were unmarried and felt they were mistaken to give up marriage since it could have saved them from their present unhappiness at work. They saw themselves as cold and domineering, "forced by painful experience to become what they were."[23]

The two groups also differed in how they viewed the years of intense career concentration. The top twenty-five made a conscious effort to deal with the sense of loss. They blamed neither their organizations nor the men and women they worked with. They realized they had made their own decisions. The other women blamed the organization and their coworkers for their unhappy lot in life, and they felt empty and used.

The personal crisis of the Harmony phase was costly to the top twenty-five, with various ones describing the transition as unhappy or depressing. The intensity of the internal struggle expended great energy. But all were satisfied with what they gained at the end of the crisis—internal quiet.

The question needs to be asked, though, Why did the top twenty-five face the crisis and why did the others never experience it? Hennig and Jardim suggest two reasons: The twenty-five had male coworkers who offered support, respect and security. Their environment helped instill courage. Also, they seemed to have an inner strength based on childhood experiences in which risk and adventure were advocated in the midst of warmth and security.

All twenty-five women in middle-management came from families where they were treated like sons. Some even had male names. They developed a "buddy" style with male colleagues to help establish their credentials. The problem was, each year their buddies became younger as the men moved on to other positions while the women remained behind. They missed the midlife crisis altogether.

These women saw themselves in an ongoing state of crisis that was not of their own making. They felt helpless. From beginning to end they never clearly understood themselves as women. Having missed that foundational understanding, they never made peace with themselves.

Standing Not Alone

The hope for the Christian woman is that, regardless what her environment is like, she can turn to God to learn how to express herself as a woman in a career and to arrive at the Harmony phase. Plus, the Bible offers us models of people who depended on God to overcome crisis.

For example, David experienced trauma after Samuel privately anointed him king while Saul was still in power (1 Samuel 16—23). Shortly after being anointed, David's father sent him as a delivery boy to supply bread and grain to his brothers, who were off playing "soldier" against the Philistines. As young David stood about with the Israelite soldiers, battle was in the air. Even though the men were garbed for war, their faces were shrouded in fear. The giant Goliath had stood like a monument in the early morning sun and issued his challenge to fight one Israelite. No one dared respond.

David milled about with the mumbling, embarrassed men, until his brother Eliab stomped up and took his aggressions out on David rather than Goliath: "What a conceited lout! What are you doing here among us men instead of watching the sheep like a boy should?"

Undaunted by his brothers, David found strength in God, risked all and accepted Goliath's challenge. Soon he found himself standing with his foot on the dead Goliath's chest.

From that single-handed victory, David's life became a cycle of military feats, increasing popularity and increasing enmity with Saul. As Saul became more threatening, David turned to the One who could strengthen him.

And God did more for David than grant him military victories. As David moved through this difficult phase, God gave him friends who loved him. His wife Michal displayed loyalty and love by helping him escape from Saul, and she faced Saul's wrath alone. David's older brother Eliab—and the rest of David's family—rallied 'round David and lived in a cave with him. That's loyalty that heartens a weary soul!

But Jonathan, Saul's son, stands out as the special gift from God. He stuck with David through his father's wrath and loved David with admirable tenacity. First Samuel 23:16 summarizes well Jonathan's contribution to David's pilgrimage to the throne. While David was still in exile, "Saul's son Jonathan went to David at Horesh and helped him find strength in God."

I believe God wants to encourage each of us to press on as we move through life's difficult passages. God wants to give us support and strength as we watch his intricate, fascinating and faithful unwinding of events that will bring us to the end he intends for us. And he wants to strengthen us through relationships, just as he did David.

God doesn't intend for us to continue to strive to be something he never planned, which is just what we do when we become absorbed in the Masculine Masquerade or when we are Occupied with the Occupation. He has much more for us. He has Harmony.

No More Acting

In my own life, I can see these three phases, yet my odyssey is not yet completed. I've been in the process of finding Harmony for several years but haven't reached the point of rest. I still have to deal with aspects of my identity.

Without making a conscious choice to place the male aspects of my person in the forefront, I did just that for the first ten years of my career. Then it occurred to me that perhaps I had forgotten how to express some important aspects of myself because I was so absorbed in my job and its reponsibilities.

I began to make a conscious effort to find out what it really meant to *me* to be feminine. I hadn't discarded any of the outward trappings of femininity; wearing bracelets and having curls were fine with me. But I realized it was the inward qualities I needed to concentrate on. I projected a strong, dominating image and appeared emotionally cool. (Actually, I was fraught with emotions but highly controlled.)

I needed to be more vulnerable by expressing my emotions as well as my thoughts and letting people see me in turmoil. I'd always been willing to express lessons learned through some travail, but peers and subordinates never knew of my internal disquiet *while* the struggle progressed. They would be amazed as I would recount to them months later some crisis in my life. Even though they had worked with me every day, they had no inkling of what was going on inside. I kept it all neatly tucked in a convenient corner of my person when I was with others. But at night, as I crawled into bed, my struggles came to life.

One humorous method God used to pry me open emotionally was the birth of six pups at our household. I had tolerated the mother dog, who belonged to one of my roommates, before the pups were born. Keeping emotional distance from dogs had never been hard for me. But before the puppies were old enough to move to new homes, one of them captured my heart, an event which was quite outside my tight and ordered plan of life. My friends couldn't believe I was hugging and petting and gushing over a dog! I ended up keeping the pup, and becoming more emotionally open because of it.

The next step was to achieve greater vulnerability with people, a process I'm still growing in. A couple of years ago, I was asked to serve on a panel to discuss singleness. My father claims that if given the opportunity to be in front of a group, I'll never say no. That must be true, because for some inexplicable reason I agreed to join the panel!

As the five of us moved to our places on the platform, I looked out at the audience of a hundred people. I quaked. Maybe I should have said no to being in front of *this* group, I thought. Then two other realizations occurred to me: the moderator was a man I felt very attracted to, and we consistently disagreed about how to define our relationship; the fellow sitting next to me on the panel was a guy I kept hoping would ask me out so I could forget the moderator. This panel, I decided, definitely was a mistake.

I thought about fainting or claiming instant tongue paralysis. But the questions were starting: How do you deal with lust? How do you handle situations in which you care for someone and that person doesn't care for you? (And there was my "uncaring" male friend moderating the discussion!)

Obviously I lived to tell the tale, but I was so emotionally exhausted by the time the panel ended, walking out of the room seemed impossible. I don't have one remembrance of how I answered a single question. Vulnerability, I was learning, was especially painful to the uninitiated. But I also felt triumphant. I had admitted I had feelings. True, with a bit more foresight and a bit less conceit, I could have picked a less threatening situation than a roomful of strangers plus two important men. Still I came away determined that vulnerability was good and that I needed more of it.

Cement Block Emotions

That day I began to learn that acting emotionally like a cement block is not only a pernicious lie but also unhealthy. I was meant to share my humanity with others and to encourage them to share their humanness with me. I'm tired of pretending I'm untouched by the turmoils of life; I don't want to simper through my traumas anymore. *That's* freedom.

I've also decided to work hard at being vulnerable with men. I've chosen not to be so concerned with protecting myself.

That's a much tougher assignment than vulnerability with wom-
en, especially being open with single men. The issue of marriage can slip in because I am concerned about the realities of
being in my thirties and unmarried. But I know that freely
expressing my emotions and being vulnerable are requirements for successfully negotiating the hairpin turns of a marriage. So I'm concentrating on learning how to be me—sometimes angry, sometimes frustrated, sometimes jealous, sometimes generous, sometimes joyful, sometimes needy—and saying I'm those things at the moment, not later. If I come out of
my crisis able to say, with the twenty-five successful women, that
I'm in harmony with myself as a woman, I will have won if I
have a husband or not.

The lives of the women studied by Hennig and Jardim, and
my own life, reflect a truth: Even though a woman may present
herself in a strongly masculine mode, underneath the straight
seams and dark colors beats the heart of a feminine person, not
an androgynous one.

If you are a woman in a male world and you have *not* experienced these phases of growth and difficulty, that could be
attributed to one of three reasons: (1) you may not be intensely
involved in your career; (2) you may have a strong system of
other women in your life who constitute role models in womanly career behavior; or (3) you may have men in your work
environment who encourage womanly expression.

Finding those support systems will help you find yourself. A
professor of management at the University of Wisconsin says
that the "different one" (the woman in management) should
receive support from male managers and other women "so that
the difference can be accepted, valued and amalgamated rather
than melted away."[24]

In his book *Man and Woman in Christ*, Stephen Clark asserts,
"According to Genesis 1, God wants both men and women."[25]
A society benefits when the differences are not only noted but

also lauded. When that happens, Margaret Mead predicts:

> We shall be ready to synthesize both kinds of gifts in the
> sciences, which are sadly lop-sided with their far greater
> knowledge of how to destroy than of how to construct, far
> better equipped to analyze the world of matter into which
> man can project his intelligence than the world of human
> relations, which requires the socialized use of intuition. . . .
> The skill of one sex gives only a partial answer. We can build
> a whole society only by using both the gifts special to each
> sex and those shared by both sexes—by using the gifts of the
> whole of humanity.[26]

Our task then becomes to understand what those gifts are.

Making It Personal

1. Express your view of male and female through circles,
boxes, continuums and so on, or choose one of the figures in
this chapter to represent your view. What effect will your view
have on your career? on your perception of your peers? on your
perception of your supervisor?

Are you comfortable with your view and its consequences? Is
there anything in your view you need to change?

2. Indicate where you think you are in the three career
phases on the continuum:

Masculine Masquerade	Occupied with the Occupation	Harmony

What struggles caused you to place yourself where you did?
Who can you turn to for help as you work your way through
the phases? Who will offer support, respect and security?

Write your own psalm, expressing belief in God's plans to
bring you to Harmony.

PART 2

Bringing
Out
Your Best

CHAPTER 6

A Woman's Strengths

Place a check mark in front of each line that describes you:

- ☐ Depend on someone else for my primary sense of security
- ☐ Try to please at all times
- ☐ Try to avoid all arguments
- ☐ Need external approval to maintain a sense of worth
- ☐ Try to maintain harmony at all costs
- ☐ Cannot express anger
- ☐ Can be extremely skilled and competent, but tend to discredit myself
- ☐ Experience guilt quickly and often
- ☐ Am quick to assume blame
- ☐ Am other-centered
- ☐ Express opinions apologetically
- ☐ Place my own needs second to those of family and others

☐ Am nonassertive in many respects
☐ Meet many of my needs through indirect and often hidden means
☐ Hesitate to accept leadership roles
☐ Work behind the scenes[1]

If you checked 0-4 lines, consider yourself strong, self-assured and possibly even stubborn; 5-8, you're a fairly confident person but cautious in stating your opinions, for you realize that even one unknown fact can make all the difference; 9-12, you're sensitive to the opinions of others, usually ready to reconsider your position when any questions—valid or not—are raised about your stand; 13-16, you fall in the traditional woman category, slow to state your opinion, quick to change it, and ready to stand behind others, for you prefer to be backstage.

Discouraged at the number of items you found true of yourself? Pleased there were so few? Hold it! Is it possible that the list contains only positive qualities—expressed in negative ways? Is it possible that the qualities are important, even integral to a woman's being an effective leader?

I think the answer is yes. Take, for example, number one: "Depends on someone else for my primary sense of security." Dependence is viewed as a negative, especially for a leader. We expect the dependent person to be a leaner, not someone we can lean on. But I contend that dependency is an abused quality. Let's look at it from a different angle.

In this quality resides a strong relational side. In its extreme form, others are everything—I can do nothing without help. But combined with a stronger sense of self, dependency becomes an interest in, involvement with, and openness to others. Doesn't concern for and respect for others appeal to us in a leader? Don't we respond to leaders who can work *with* us? Don't we all long for a leader who really listens when, in a tumble of words, we try to describe a concept that could transform our work situation? Don't we want to know that our boss respects us as individuals? This positive trait is the flip side of dependency. The same could be said for every trait on the test.

What Happened to Woman?

If that is true—if each characteristic on this test of femininity has a positive side—why don't we often see that side? The answer goes back a long way, to when the first people were created. Life was very different.

We can't really imagine an unflawed life: relating to one another without insecurity but with zealous oneness, relating to God as an intimate acquaintance, having no sense of inadequacy, knowing no fear. Such congruence exceeds our comprehension.

We know little of what life was like for Adam and Eve during their stint in the Garden. We do know that God created man and woman equal and unflawed and that they worked, maybe taking time out now and then to play leapfrog.

"So God created man in his own image, in the image of God he created him; male and female he created them" (Genesis 1:27). The Hebrew word for "image," *selem,* means a copy or counterpart; it signifies equality for both the man and the woman, who were made in God's image.[2]

And God created them for intimacy. Singular and plural are used to refer to God in the creation account: "Let *us* . . . in *our* image" (Genesis 1:26); *"his* own image" (Genesis 1:27). Singular and plural also refer to humanity in verse 27 "created *him* . . . created *them."* Both instances show relationships. God is three in one—all equal and all God. Mankind is a duality of male and female—both equal and both human. Both are created as a unique reflection of God and both are designed to relate to him. Male is not a full reflection of God nor is female. Both are needed to reflect God's image and to make up humanity.

The humans are given commands to follow: "Be fruitful . . . and rule over" (v. 28). As God's image, Adam and Eve are given the privilege of doing God's work—creating life and ruling over it. Because woman is given the same injunction as man, apparently work, or "rule," is equally important to her.[3]

So it becomes Adam and Eve's responsibility to divvy up the duties as they see fit. How do you suppose they decided? Maybe Adam got the job of cleaning out the pigsty the day he had a stuffed nose; Eve gathered the fruit from the trees because she was taller. However that all worked out, Adam and Eve expressed their unflawed abilities in tending their environment and in creating life.

Then came their shattering choice to disobey God and to eat the forbidden fruit. Their act shattered life, their relationship with God, their relationship with each other, and their individual personalities. Wherever there had been togetherness there was now brokenness. Perfect maleness and femaleness disintegrated.

Adam and Eve's task, and ours too, suddenly changed. They still needed to tend to the environment and procreate, but now they needed to put themselves together again, to try to find wholeness again, to learn to express their bent (flawed) qualities in straight ways.

God did not leave Adam and Eve, or us, alone to put ourselves together again. He searched through the Garden to find his emotionally and spiritually bruised children. When he found them hiding he gave them a promise and a hope: after death comes resurrection; after brokenness, wholeness. And he planted seeds of remembrance throughout nature so they—and we—wouldn't forget. In nature life is renewed. Spring unfolds from winter. A seed stuck into the damp ground later pushes up in new life. And, of course, God provided the ultimate hope in another death and resurrection—Jesus'.

The Task of Eve
So our work became learning how to find wholeness in our

individual lives, how to transform weakness into strength, how to mend our femaleness.

Sometimes I weary of the task of Eve, of repairing my fractured femaleness. But then I recall two resurrection promises God has given me. One is in Scripture: "Being confident of this, that he who began a good work in you will carry it on to completion" (Philippians 1:6). Real completion, of course, will be in eternity, but God has determined we will progress to that end and keep moving to completion starting in this life.

The other resurrection promise hangs from my living room ceiling. It's a gray pottery mobile of doves. It signifies God's power to transform brokenness into beauty, and weakness into strength, just as the artist took blobs of clay and made them into doves of peace. My students presented it to me after I had spent a couple of class sessions telling them about the work toward wholeness within ourselves and our relationships. My sessions included several examples from my life about the death of relationships. They were hard for me to talk about because I still grieved the loss.

The student who presented the mobile to me said, "Thank you for showing us through your life that God wants to take the broken and remake it into something new and beautiful. This mobile represents that lesson."

Some days when I despair over the work of becoming, my eyes catch sight of the mobile. And I remember God's past faithfulness and his promise to complete what he has begun.

I know God wants us to be whole women, celebrating what he made us. He doesn't want us to remain broken. Our task is to decide which parts of us to celebrate and which parts to work with God to transform.

Every Woman a Leader?
Transforming weakness to strength does not mean that every woman would be a leader if only she expressed her innate

femininity in unbent ways. Even with all their weaknesses turned into strengths, some women would still be most comfortable in the kitchen. And that's fine.

But because women tend not to be found in leadership positions, we conclude they must have the wrong qualities. Women deny they have strengths that men don't have—and vice versa. Women have sought to change themselves to match a male expression of leadership. We've accepted the lie that male is best; maleness is to be displayed by everyone. But that's a denial of what God made us. By exalting maleness, Janet Giele states, the "American culture [has arrived] at the breaking point, victim of an overly 'male' emphasis that teaches a relentless desire to dominate nature, repress feelings, and pursue 'success' at all costs."[4]

But even as we attempt to reassess our womanhood, a specter raises its ghostly head. Women have been taught they cannot make it as leaders if they refuse to forfeit some of their womanliness. We have been taught that womanly qualities are not assets in careers; they are liabilities. And unwritten rules of acceptable behavior describe *masculine* behavior.

Studies show that on the job workers earn "idiosyncracy credits." Only after conforming to required behavior for a period of time does the worker achieve the right to violate the norms.[5] It's like having a restricted bank account. Only after a certain number of deposits can you make a withdrawal.

Because a woman working in a male environment is already violating tradition, she must conform in many more work expectations before she is allowed to deviate. That expectation of high conformity, of course, places women in conflict with the environment and with themselves. Some women discover, as did the twenty-five top executives mentioned in the previous chapter, that the pressure to conform squeezes out their femininity. Many of these women eventually decide to be feminine. They realize femaleness is an undeniable aspect of themselves.

But women shouldn't have to backtrack to find where they dumped their womanliness. It should never be cast aside for the sake of becoming "professional."

Ending Conflict

Ultimately, this merry-go-round grinds to a halt when the woman decides that she's going to be herself. No compromises, no guesses as to what others want, just who she is, a flawed but female reflection of her Creator. Anne Ulanov states it well:

A woman receiving all of herself carries with her the conviction that you do not come to yourself either by subtraction or abstraction. To call feminine only those qualities of compassion and nurture traditionally associated with woman omits essential pieces of a woman's reality—power, intellect, aggression. To take away from a woman her vaunted softness and interiority, leaving only capacities for anger and a warrior-like boldness, equally distorts her reality, abstracting and concentrating on one kind of element to define a much larger whole.[6]

But how does a woman express those elusive aspects of herself? How does she combine them with leadership?

I have categorized those qualities which most women possess and which are most frequently seen as liabilities in the workplace—those traits that get tucked away in a corner of her briefcase by the professional woman. I believe those traits are vulnerability, generosity, flexibility, cooperativeness and connectedness. Together, in the next five chapters, I will explore those qualities, looking at how we have misshapen them because of our imperfections and how we can reshape them into assets.

But first, we need to cast aside two myths: (1) that nothing but lucky breaks and a certain boldness separate the woman in leadership from the woman who follows; and (2) that one leadership style will win for every woman.

Set Apart

Tests clearly show that a woman in leadership is as capable of displaying traditional feminine qualities as other females, but she outscores them in self-confidence, achievement, dominance and nurturing (defined as being "helpful to others, dependable and benevolent").[7] She shows more independence than women in general, with leanings toward the thinking rather than the feeling side of life.[8]

But, in comparison to her male peers, she is more sensitive to the feelings of others and more intelligent. She's weaker than men in ego strength, displaying less confidence and less will power. Probably much of this seeming insecurity comes from living "out of context."[9]

The professional woman finds herself in no man's (or is it person's?) land, psychologically somewhere between women in general and men. One researcher concluded that these women need to "give up male standards, judgments, and views of what is permissible for them . . . daring to be autonomous and self-assertive without fear of criticism."[10]

Women in leadership are intelligent, versatile and gifted. No mere luck nor brassiness gave them their positions—talent placed them there. By the same token, talent and intelligence must tell them how best to be a woman in their particular circumstances.

Pick a Posture

One work style is not correct, comfortable and practical for all women. After interviewing sixty successful women, Jane Adams came to the conclusion that there are many successful styles. Perhaps more so for women than for men, whose directions are more clearly marked by a society that tells them how best to succeed. Faced with unique needs, a stringent cultural role, and biology, the successful woman finds her own route.[11]

One management style some women find comfortable is playing the big sister. Dorothy Crouch of Warner Brothers, who adopted this style, says, "I always had two younger brothers, whom I was left to babysit. It never occurred to me that I couldn't control them, and some of that carried over to business."[12]

Female leaders come in lots of different flavors. I tested ten women leaders in Christian organizations and found they fell into two seemingly opposite categories: "dominant" and "compliant."[13] (Seven tested as dominant and three as compliant.) The dominant personality places emphasis on shaping her environment by overcoming opposition, while the compliant person emphasizes working with existing conditions to produce quality. The women were all high in independence and discipline.

Those who were compliant were in more structured and longer-established positions than the other women. Many of the seven dominants were the first in their jobs, displaying more of a pioneer spirit. Job type and personality type (dominant = pioneer job; compliant = structured position) seemed to be the key in their leadership styles. Of course, I'm well aware that testing ten women does not create valid statistics. My point is that these women were all leaders, and each had found a management style that suited her personality.

Corporate personalities vary too. A wise woman will seek out an organization that is attuned to her leadership style. The chart on the next page divides corporations into three "personality" types.[14]

A person decides the environment she is most compatible with and finds a corporation that matches the description. I, for example, could handle a leader's position in a collegial organization but would probably be happiest in a personalistic environment. I'd either blow up the building of any formalistic corporation that foolishly hired me or spend my emotional energies working to create a collegial atmosphere. For some-

Three Types of Organizational Culture

	Formalistic	*Collegial*	*Personalistic*
Basis for Decision	Direction from authority	Discussion, agreement	Directions from within
Form of Control	Rules, laws, rewards, punishments	Interpersonal, group commitments	Actions aligned with self-concept
Source of Power	Superior	What "we" think and feel	What I think and feel
Desired End	Compliance	Consensus	Self-actualization
To Be Avoided	Deviation from authoritative direction; taking risks	Failure to reach consensus	Not being "true to oneself"
Time Perspective	Future	Near Future	Now
Position Relative to Others	Hierarchical	Peer	Individual
Human Relationships	Structured	Group oriented	Individually oriented
Basis for Growth	Following the established order	Peer group membership	Acting on awareness of self

one else, the formalistic organization would fit just right.

When it comes to work styles, labels aren't important; development of your person is. Most women develop their style as they encounter everyday circumstances and formulate a few foundational decisions. A new position opens for you. You find yourself making decisions about situations you never encountered before: Should I hire Pat or Peg? Is it ethical to make this statement in our next brochure just because we plan for it to be true? How can I get the finances to pull off this project? Should I accept the reserved parking-lot space or fend for a space like everyone else?

You find yourself scouting out a comfortable, honest and ethical route for that moment, for that decision. But it all adds up to a basic stance. Part of the criteria in your decision making must be the image you hold of yourself and how you want your coworkers to see you.

Like me, some women sense from the first that they can't consciously emulate men—that isn't comfortable. And they aren't going to play mother—that's ridiculous. I sensed that for me the answer lay somewhere between those two postures. Maybe big sister is a good way to describe the role I have in mind for myself. The phrase encompasses the warmth of a sister and yet the emotional distance inherent in being the "big" sister. But it's a label, not a stiff, high-sided box. One manager, who was called Mother Jane by her employees, didn't see herself as a mother-image. But that name was okay because it meant her people saw that she cared about them.

No Boxes, Please
In an effort to stave off easy labeling of herself, a woman needs to decide what characteristics are most important for her to display in her working relationships. Care and servanthood must be cornerstones as she constructs her philosophy of leadership, especially as a Christian. And those are attitudes that a Christian woman should be especially strong in displaying—because she is a woman and because she is a Christian.

For me, I also opted to always choose the person over the product. That means taking risks to protect my people from misuse. I tried to remember that someday God would ask me about my decisions and how they affected people. My goal was to envision myself responding to his queries without stammering, or averting my eyes, or feeling I needed to explain the intricacies of the situation so he could grasp why I acted as I did. If I realized I would be uncomfortable in explaining my

decision to him, I needed to give more thought to the matter—
and probably needed to reverse my decision.

Connie, who works on a church staff with seventy volunteers
reporting to her, believes sincere praise is key to her leadership
style. "But I'll never flatter," she says. "I've seen church leaders
manipulate people to serve the church through false praise. I
want to care about people more than about what they can do
for me." Connie carefully picked a fluid managerial style while
taking a leadership class in seminary. If there's high anxiety or
a lot of foot dragging, she takes a dominant stance. But if group
members are internally motivated and responsible, she remains
low-key and lets the team move on its own impetus.

She displays several of the following qualities, which are
deemed imperative in a good manager and therefore are important to reflect in any leadership style: a high sense of responsibility and commitment, the ability to cope with ambiguity,
a continuing sense of curiosity, and a willingness to learn.[15]

Other research on qualities found in successful managers
showed that effective managers tend to be social initiators; they
anticipate problems and possible solutions. They also build alliances, bring people together and develop networks. And they
possess talents in several areas, including social and emotional
maturity (composed of such traits as self-control, spontaneity,
perceptual objectivity, accurate self-assessment, stamina, adaptability); *entrepreneurial abilities* (logical thought, conceptual ability, the diagnostic use of ideas and memory); and *interpersonal
abilities* (self-preservation, interest in the development of others,
concern with impact, oral communication skills, the use of so-
cialized power, and concern with relationships).[16]

Neither sex has a monopoly on those characteristics. Ultimately, regarding good leadership, we must recognize:

It would be a grave error to conceive of executive success as
dependent on toughness or softness, assertiveness or sensitivity, masculinity or femininity. That popular delusion has

already caused too much damage, both to individuals who are impersonating males and females, and to the institutions for which they work.[17]

Develop your own style, which is a reflection of the leanings God has given you, and seek to place yourself with an organization that uses those strengths. Remember that an integral part of your personhood is your sexual identity. It brings with it certain characteristics, many of which, when expressed positively, serve as assets.

Putting It into Practice

1. Turn to the italicized list of qualities of an effective manager on page 84. Underline the traits you think are true of you. If you find less than half are true, leadership may not be your strength. More than three-fourths shows you have leadership gifts that are important to use wisely.

2. Study your present supervisor's modus operandi for two weeks. Keep a list of qualities you'd like to emulate and those you'd rather avoid. Be careful not to be judgmental. You just might be in that position someday and long for your subordinates to remember that you're human, too.

3. As you study your supervisor, think and pray about foundational principles you always want to be true for you as a leader. (Mine are (a) be a caring servant; (b) choose people over product.) Try to write out your principles in succinct mottoes or phrases to help you recall them when the pressure is on. Develop just a few. You'll find even working on two can strain every fiber of your being.

4. Do a study in Scripture on your principle(s). A word study (e.g., servant) might get you started, or study Jesus' life, looking for ways he lived out your principle. Ask God to embed in your heart a zeal to cling to your principles no matter what.

CHAPTER 7

Open Communication

Women are the decorative sex," Oscar Wilde declared. "They never have anything to say, but they say it charmingly." Tests do show that women differ from men in communicating, but not necessarily along the lines of Wilde's suggestion.

We have discussed the conflicts a woman faces as she takes on responsibility and works at a career. We have looked at the very real differences between men and women and how career women often express their feminine characteristics as weaknesses rather than strengths. Now we want to take a look at some typically feminine traits and see how those traits might help a woman to be a good worker, leader or manager. Of course, I'm making generalizations here. These traits are ways in which *most* women differ from *most* men. But not all women possess these characteristics nor do all men lack them.

Who Talks More

The first characteristic we will look at is *vulnerability*, especially in communication. Which of the following statements about communication do you think are true and which false?

☐ Men talk more than women.

☐ Men interrupt women more than women interrupt men.

☐ Women have one more pitch of intonation than men.

☐ Men use more hostile verbs in speaking.

☐ Women use more supportive verbs.

If you decided that all the answers were true, then you're in agreement with communication studies.[1]

In addition to the differences brought out in the test above, women also (more often than men) vary how open they will be in a particular situation. This suggests that women are more sensitive to their surroundings when determining what to disclose. Also, women portray and perceive emotions more effectively than men in group interaction. In nonverbal communication, women strive for greater eye contact than men, perhaps in an effort to receive a maximum number of nonverbal cues.[2]

Each of these communication traits emanates from one of women's greatest strengths: the willingness to disclose oneself and to be sensitive to others. Women tend to bring to relationships a seemingly odd blend of elements: dependence, interdependence, and independence. All three woven together form a fabric of vulnerability. Women want mutual dependence in relationships. But women also seek independence and a strong sense of personhood; an awareness of one's uniqueness. If we lack this, then a close relationship will be threatening. We'll feel smothered.

This ability to be vulnerable is a woman's special strength. That doesn't mean men can't be open and vulnerable; it does mean women are more prone to be so, and they work to maintain openness in their relationships. Openness and vulnerability strengthen and cement relationships. It's a plus on the job and off, with individuals and groups. Of course, different levels of vulnerability are appropriate in various types of relationships.

A Time to Speak

Here are two simple questions to ask yourself as an opportunity to be open about yourself arises. Will my openness build up the other person? Will it enhance the relationship? If the answer to even one of the questions is yes, we should respond with courage and speak up. But if the answer is no, then opt for silence. Often vulnerability means exposing our own frailties. But spoken in the right manner, these revelations build up others as we trust them with our imperfections.

Susan, for example, handled a tough situation by being vulnerable with her supervisor. She was assigned to edit a new promotional piece—a newsletter—for her company. Two male consultants were called in to help get the publication going. They expressed through words and action, that, in their opinion, Susan was an unfortunate element in their job. Instead of treating her like the editor, they acted as though she were their secretary. They let it be known they were highly qualified, and in their opinion Susan, despite her years of experience, was not.

Susan responded by letting them know she thought they were fools. She never actually said so, but her intent was clear. And her attitude made the situation worse. So she decided to talk to her supervisor, Phil, about the conflicts. She admitted she had not handled the circumstances gracefully, but she was in despair as to how to work with the men.

Phil and Susan respected one another, and he received Susan's anger and frustration with empathy. He talked to the men about his intention to keep Susan in her job, and he encouraged her to respond with grace to her two egotistical colleagues.

In such situations, when you feel threatened, it's tough to be honest about your feelings. And it's tempting to decide just to keep them to yourself. But because Susan talked to Phil, their relationship grew. Of course, she was fortunate that she had a close relationship with her boss. And he responded well to her, encouraging her to work her way through the problems. Not every supervisor has that sort of insight and therefore sometimes such openness can lead to trouble.

Sometimes husbands and wives struggle with the woman's greater capacity for vulnerability.[3] Stan was promoted to a demanding new job. He was highly pleased, but just before he began his new responsibilities, he started showing physical symptoms of stress. Sensing that the new job was worrying him, Stan's wife, Jennifer, suggested that Stan hire someone to help with the yard work in the summer so Stan could give his energies to the new job. But this suggestion made him angry. Later Stan admitted to himself, and then to Jennifer, that he was feeling overwhelmed. But hiring help was too much of an admission of weakness.

In this situation, Jennifer's sensitivity and willingness to be vulnerable by making a constructive suggestion were not rewarded. Instead, she was dealt with in anger.

Even if women are encouraged to display vulnerability, it's usually to tune into the emotions and reactions of others, as Jennifer did with Stan. But then women become diverted from examining and expressing their own emotions. In this way, they demonstrate how their femininity is bent and how their vulnerability can be a weakness.

Women need to apply their highly developed faculty to understand themselves as well as others. They need to be in touch with their own emotions.

Such was the case for Marilyn, who found herself under more stress than she could handle. The stress came from the uncooperative students in the high-school English class she taught, from her disintegrating marriage, and from her troubled teen-age daughter. Not knowing how to handle these pressures, she decided to see a psychologist.

Marilyn could tell the psychologist that Peter was probably her prime problem in the classroom because of the hurt and confusion he felt over the death of his younger brother. She understood that her husband's masculinity was deeply threatened because she had to work to help out financially. And she comprehended the deep-seated insecurities her daughter felt because Marilyn's husband had always been unemotional and physically distant from the girl.

But when the psychologist asked, "What are *you* feeling?" Marilyn could only respond with a furrowed brow. She had been so busy understanding everyone else that she didn't understand herself.

Feeling Good

The key is not to bury your emotions but to deal with them in productive and healthy ways. Anger is an especially debilitating emotion that creates internal havoc if it's not expressed. But many Christians think that anger is a sin and therefore must never be expressed. The sin is not the feeling of anger but what often accompanies it—the impugning of another person, the harboring of bitterness and resentment, the unforgiving spirit, or the stiff pride. In my life, I've committed these sins far more consistently because I *didn't* deal with my anger.

Anger is an emotion that God himself expressed. It's attributed to him more than to anyone else in the Bible—220 times. But his anger is more than hot air; it's controlled, articulate, and aimed at correcting a situation. It is used in a positive way.

Exodus 34:6 describes him as a "compassionate and gracious God, slow to anger, abounding in love and faithfulness." That doesn't mean he never experiences and never expresses anger, but it's balanced with other qualities—compassion, graciousness, lovingkindness and truth. The same should be true of us, for then anger becomes an integral part of our vulnerability.

When we women feel angry, too vulnerable and pressed in, we have learned to speak in generalities rather than stern logic with the facts organized. Words like *should* and *ought* start proliferating in our conversations. My personal pet phrase is *not right*—"It's not right for her to report a peer for that infraction of a silly rule." When I'm angry, everything starts falling to the right or left of some invisible line that demarcates right and wrong, should and should not, ought and ought not.

Psychologist Anne Ulanov suggests that women need to learn to accept their ire as authentic and then offer "an articulate anger" rather than "defensive opinionizing."[4] In other words, a woman needs to learn to explain logically *why* she is angry rather than venting her emotions in a stream of heated generalities that seem impossible to comprehend.

When Susan finally expressed her frustration to her boss, she didn't say, "I'm never going to work with those men again." That's a hot generality, not a specific statement. "He shouldn't have talked to me that way," doesn't exactly pinpoint the problem either. "I felt unappreciated and angry when he told me the front-page article was colorless," moves closer to the heart of the matter. The chart below shows the difference between articulate and inarticulate anger:

Articulate anger is not:	*Articulate anger is:*
☐ Blowing up.	☐ Carefully explaining why I'm upset about the incident.
☐ Maligning the other person—and saying things I'm going to regret.	☐ Remembering in the midst of my emotion that I do care about the other person—centering the discussion on the *event* that has caused me anger.
☐ Saying, "You always . . ."	☐ Saying, "I feel . . ."

I personally have discovered that it's freeing to be honest enough to say, "I'm angry." It releases the mounting tension within me and helps the other person respond to what I'm experiencing. But it took me time to feel comfortable in making that statement. At first I had a friend who would ask me how I felt about an upsetting situation. I would say, "I'm hurt."

"Are you angry?"

"Just hurt." That always ended the discussion.

But finally I realized she kept asking me those questions for a reason—she was right. I *was* angry. But acknowledging anger didn't mean I knew how to express it. Instead, I would seethe. "I'm so *ticked* that he said that to me," I'd mutter with folded arms and gritted teeth.

Learning to Be Wrathful

Then God placed a friend in my life who recognized my advanced case of controlled emotions. I was sensitive to everyone's feelings but my own. Wayne kept telling me I could say anything to him. Then one day he promised to phone me later when we both had more time to talk. I had had a tough day and wanted to tell him all. But he never called.

I decided to test the water and expressed dismay the next day. Wayne accepted it and apologized for not calling. Gee, that was pretty easy.

A few weeks later, I was explaining a deep hurt to him, and he responded in what I considered a cavalier fashion. That really hurt. I got mad. So I lambasted him with the gale force of my anger and hurt, listing all the specifics. He received it all and acknowledged how right I was and how wrong he'd been.

Immediately my face fell. I realized, once I'd vented my anger, that I had castigated Wayne not just because his comments were so upsetting but because I was angry at God, another friend, and my boss. (It had been a bad week.) Wayne just happened to say the wrong thing at the wrong time and ended up receiving my railing for *all* the Bad Guys in my life.

His response to my mumbled apology was a hallmark in my emotional growth. He smiled, touched my arm, and said, "Janet, you don't trust our relationship enough to *really* believe it's okay to be angry. We're seldom isolated in our anger. I can handle any degree of anger you can give out, and I *was* wrong in what I said."

So, with the encouragement of a caring friend, I found more freedom to express my anger. And I learned to make it articulate ("Why did you say _____ ? What I needed to hear was _____ .") I not only vented an authentic emotion, but we also ended up closer friends who trusted each other more.

After an upsetting situation, it's helpful to objectify the event before you respond to it, if you can stall for time to do so. A helpful device is to write out the facts. Recall on paper how the upsetting situation unfolded and attempt to come to grips with why you and the other parties responded as you did. Ask yourself if you need to apologize. Or if you have sinned and need to confess your error to God, then admit it to those involved. Write out what positive action you can take.

Also, pray and tell your heavenly Father about it. Express just how hard and ugly the situation was for you. Then, after releasing your emotions, ask God if you've perceived the situation correctly. Ask him how he would have you respond to it. And be willing to make amends if you've offended or wronged anyone.

If there isn't time to regroup privately, admit to the group that the situation is hard for you to handle. It's time to display vulnerability, and if you do it with dignity and without casting aside logic, you may give others a new and positive view of expressing emotion. If you have to pause and cry a few tears before you can regroup, do so, and then speak the facts as you see them.

If you know that once you start crying, it's going to be a downpour, excuse yourself from the group and go out and sob. Then swallow your pride and return to the group, red nose and all, ready to talk it out.

The Foxes

We shouldn't be naive here either and always assume that if we show vulnerability by caring for others and by exposing our emotions that we'll be assured a "just" reward. In every environment foxes lurk, ready to pounce and interpret sensitivity as incompetence.

When I find myself wrongly interpreted and taken advantage of, I go straight to my Father and ask for his protection and for justice to befall my enemy. Now, sometimes God's mill of justice grinds slowly, but it grinds fine. If I'm motivated by a desire to use my innate qualities in God-honoring ways, I believe God *will* take care of me.

I saw one woman lose her job because she was "done in" by wiley foxes. But I also saw God give her a better, more fulfilling job.

On the other hand, I've seen a person display vulnerability and be pushed into a corner. She is still ignored because of that one incident. She has stayed on the job, but she consistently is passed over at promotion time and has little influence with her peers. But I say God writes his own endings to these stories. This particular story isn't ended yet.

We need to be wise in when and how we are vulnerable, but not cowed into conformity by those who want to do us in. *That's* not honoring to God.

Above all, don't squelch your emotions, and don't forget that logic has a place in life, too.

A Time to Cry

Now, even though it seems to contradict the idea of using logic while being emotional, let me tell you about the time I fell apart emotionally, and lost all my logic, and it proved to be the best thing that could have happened. Margaret and I sat in my living room not talking. Then we talked *at* each other. We had started out disagreeing about the interpretation of a movie, but that had quickly moved us on to deeper levels of frustration about how we had been relating to each other. I saw her as too demanding; she saw me as uninvolved.

We were encased in a freezer-cold discussion for what seemed like an ice age. We were making no progress in reaching agreement; we weren't even interested in trying. I sat on the couch with my arms crossed and my heart cold; Margaret assumed a similar posture in the wingback chair.

As we stared at each other, cold-eyed, it occurred to me that I was inflicting emotional lacerations, stroke by stroke, word by word, on Margaret.

But I cared about her! What was I doing? When I saw how destructive I'd become, my tears came—profuse and unstoppable. I was pained by my selfishness and stubbornness and what it was doing to someone I loved. As soon as I started sobbing, Margaret's icy pose melted. Soon she was on the couch hugging me and crying with me.

Words and logic didn't bring us together; it was my emotional deluge that melted both of us and fostered an atmosphere of forgiveness and acceptance. If I hadn't cried, I suspect she would have left with a sharp chill in the air. We would have gone into a deep freeze, with both of us stubbornly refusing to resolve the matter for who knows how long. But my sobbing brought a positive resolution to our self-imposed cold war.

So recognize that logic is wonderful to place up-front, but when emotions take charge, don't assume all is lost. It may be the best thing that could happen—even if it's embarrassing.

Our tears are important expressions of caring. One who doesn't care will not cry. Remember Jesus crying over Lazarus' death? Why did he cry? He knew he was going to raise up Lazarus even while the tears ran down his cheeks. I think he cried partly because he cared about the agony of his friends Mary and Martha.

Jesus personified what we've said about vulnerability in this chapter. He communicated to others that he cared, and therefore was outward-directed in his vulnerability. He communicated also what he felt, and therefore was inward-directed in his vulnerability, knowing his feelings and expressing them. He used his vulnerability as a strength, not a weakness, just as we should. And as women we have a special ability for doing so.

Personal Application
How would you respond if:

1. You had been working overtime for several weeks to complete a heavy load of projects. You had managed to meet all the deadlines, much to everyone's amazement. You had done B-level work, but had purposely chosen that course so you could meet all the deadlines.

Then one day you come to work and find the projects on your desk with a long reprimand from your supervisor for the quality of the work. You feel angry, overworked, unappreciated, underpaid, embarrassed and worried about your status with your boss. Just then your supervisor walks in and sees you holding the reprimand.

What are your options for response?

Which would you pick and why?

Write out the exact words you wish you would have the presence of mind to say.

2. It's four o'clock, and you're sitting in the conference room with your peers. You're discussing the content of an upcoming seminar your department will present to the rest of the company. Everyone is nervous because it's important the department look good.

You've made several suggestions throughout the day. Apparently they were good ones because, even though no one commented on them when you said them, as soon as a man restated them, everyone said a quick yes to what looked like *his* idea.

Your frustration level is high. But you say nothing. Then you think you see a solution to an especially vexing part of the seminar format. So you take a deep breath and mention your solution.

To your surprise, the fellow sitting across from you says, "That's a good idea. Could you develop that some more?"

All eyes turn to you. But the frustrations of the day and now the sudden glare of the limelight do you in. You realize you're about to cry!

What are your options?

Which would you pick and why?

What are the men's possible responses (both positive and negative) to what you would do?

CHAPTER 8

A Giving Spirit

Am I giving enough? Can I give enough? Why can't I give enough? Psychologist Jean Miller says women constantly confront themselves with these questions. The trait of a giving spirit is frequently so near to a woman's heart that it becomes a prime portion of her being.

Miller reports that women have deep fears about what this must mean about them: "They wonder what would happen if they were to stop giving, to even consider not giving."[1]

Men Who Must Do

Miller goes on to say: "Few men feel that giving is a primary issue in their struggles for identity. They are concerned much more about 'doing.' Am I a doer? Do I measure up to the proper image of someone who does?"[2] Our society enhances these roles by expecting a man to "take" a wife, while a woman "gives" herself. A man who cherishes his wife often expresses what a "gift" she is, as though she has been given to him, and that's often exactly how the wife feels.

Miller believes that many men want to give of themselves, and certainly that should be true of Christian men, but it is much harder for them to find a way to do so that will contribute to their sense of identity. "For men, giving is clearly an added luxury that is allowed only *after* they have fulfilled the primary requirements of manhood," Miller states.[3]

These points were borne out in a study designed to examine the different ways in which male and female egos function. Men sought to differentiate themselves from others; women sought to merge with others. Men intellectually were involved in separating and ordering; women in communicating. The men's interpersonal style involved objectivity, competition, exclusion and distance. The women's style centered on subjectivity, cooperation, acceptance and closeness.[4]

The desire to give is an important contribution that a woman can make to work relationships as well as personal relationships. In many ways her self-image is linked with giving to others, and her worth is enhanced as she does so.

Cherie exemplifies the special gift of giving in her position as a department manager of a large corporation. When a secretary learned her grandfather had died, it was Cherie who was thoughtful enough to ask: "How close were you to your grandfather?"

Cherie ordered flowers for the coworker who missed weeks of work because of illness. She was also the one who laughed and joked with an angry subordinate so he could relax enough to see the funny side of the situation.

With her quiet, unassuming but caring manner, Cherie brings tranquillity to a high-speed department because giving is an integral part of her style.

A giving spirit is a welcome quality at work, where everything is rushed and everyone is stressed. And, surprisingly, giving is encouraging even when it comes in small packages. In addition to Cherie's ways of giving, you can create a caring atmosphere by:

1. Writing a one-sentence note of "well done" when a subordinate finishes a project.

2. Thumbing through an old magazine and cutting out phrases and photos to create a homemade card to cheer someone who is down or to congratulate someone who is up.

3. Calling a coworker who has been sick for several days.

4. Putting an apple in the mail box (or on the desk) of a person who needs cheering.

5. Asking a question that gives the other person an opportunity to express what he or she is feeling.

6. Creating "Entertainment Logs" for a coworker's children to take on the family vacation. Simply staple some paper together with different items for the children to draw when they find them, such as the first blue thing you see on your trip; the first thing with four legs, and so on.

7. Giving a subordinate extra time off after finishing a big project. (Even getting to go home an hour early is a bonus.)

Giving is a simple gift, as these suggestions show. It's being thoughtful when it's easy to be thoughtless. Flourishes and marching bands aren't needed to make people feel appreciated and noticed. Giving is touching another person at work. In turn that person feels important and motivated to do well. Giving enhances a sense of worth and self-respect that is bound to be reflected on the job. For all its simplicity, giving has profound results.

Most women, like Cherie, don't need to teach themselves how to give; they learn it at a young age. For example, Lee, a thirty-six-year-old woman, remembers how her mother modeled the quality of giving. "When I was little, I remember my mother cutting pie. If a piece got messed up, or one piece was smaller than the others, she always took the damaged or smaller piece. So I learned to always give people the bigger part; it brought joy to me. Even now, if I get some strawberries or any special treat, I save them until I can share them with someone."

In Lee's case, however, this giving spirit began to dominate her whole life. At one point, Lee's schedule looked like this (she is single): get up and make two or three phone calls to friends to encourage them before work; write notes of encouragement during breaks at work; go to lunch with a needy friend; get home at 5:00; be out the door by 5:30 for dinner with another needy friend.

For variation, Lee wrote letters while she ate dinner in her apartment. Since she was corresponding with twenty to twenty-five people on a regular basis and fifty people sporadically, a stack of letters several inches high always pressured her to respond.

"I got so I didn't want any letters in my mail box," Lee admits. "Or sometimes when I got a letter I wouldn't open it because I knew I would have to write back. My body was rigid because I never relaxed," she says. "I was always giving." Somehow the joy of giving, which Lee had started out with, had become warped, as it does in many women's lives. It had become an obsession rather than a delight.

Attached Strings

Women are often willing to give out of self-denial rather than out of a sense of using a God-given ability. Based on a weak view of herself, a woman will be driven to bribe others to accept, like and even love her because of her giving. She can be convinced that as she consistently displays this pleasing quality, others will be drawn irresistibly to her. But even when others respond well to her giving nature, she finds herself frustrated, for she secretly realizes they have affirmed the act of giving rather than her person.

Leah, one of Jacob's wives, is an example of a woman who I think gave in hopes of return—and was frustrated in the process (Genesis 29—30). She had a reluctant husband. Her father had employed trickery to pull off their marriage, and Leah knew she was unloved. She knew she had keen competition, for Jacob richly loved his other wife, her sister Rachel. Leah attempted to win her husband by giving—by bearing him sons. This stood in sharp contrast to Rachel's early childlessness.

Leah kept hoping each son would cause her husband to have a change of heart and love her. She even named her third son Levi, meaning "attached," perhaps because she was convinced her husband would become attached to her in response to the son's birth. Even by the time her sixth son was born, she still may have held forth hope that her fertility would bring her husband's care. She named number six "Honor" (Zebulun), perhaps hoping that Jacob would honor her.

Yet always Rachel, the favorite, came first with Jacob. While traveling one time, when the family was endangered, Jacob placed Leah and her seven children behind the danger zone, and then, farther back still, came Rachel with Joseph (Genesis 33:2). Leah, for all her striving, failed to win love through giving. She had misused her strength, and it availed her nothing.

Mis-giving

Why do women become so misguided in their giving? Why do they lack the self-love to give out of the bounty within? Lee believes she became misdirected out of a poor self-image. Despite her strong, positive upbringing, she became aware of inadequacies as she grew up and began to develop relationships. If she started to tell a story, often people would interrupt her to tell their own—and they never got back to Lee's story.

So she decided she must be a boring person. Well, what's a boring person to do if she wants to relate to others? Learn to be a great listener. People would have intense conversations while all Lee did was ask questions. She seldom revealed anything about herself or what she thought because others didn't express an interest in learning about her.

She remembers imagining that when she got before God she would say, "I helped other people to develop their gifts." But she had a haunting, recurring nightmare that when she got to the throne, God would say, "There were things I meant you to be but you never became them because you were so busy parceling out your time here and there like small gifts."

Giving is a good and godly gift, but a woman must be sure that her giving is based on an expression of her self-worth and her sincere interest in others. We should give out of self-love. Jesus endorsed this when he insisted that we love others as we love ourselves.

So much of the essence of giving has its basis in self-love. Not self-centeredness which tries to win favor, but a strong sense of personal worth. Gladys Hunt says it well:

> Every person needs to be convinced of her intrinsic worth, lest she spend her life denying it or trying to prove it, both of which are wasteful and selfish. . . . Intrinsic means *belonging to a thing by its very nature.* We have been made in the image of God.[5]

Hunt points out that Hagar, Sarah's servant who bore a child for Abraham, probably came to realize the basis for her real worth through some harrowing experiences.

> A slave, bearing a child for her master, then being sent away because of jealousy—used, abused, desperate, deserted. And then the voice of God from heaven, "What troubles you, Hagar? Fear not, for God . . ." We are not dispensable to God. We are unworthy, yes. But we are not worthless. . . . We will look . . . for hundreds of other ways to feel good about

ourselves, and none of them will be as validating as worth found in the heart of God.[6]

That means we don't *have* to give. Dr. Miller states:

As wives, mothers, daughters, lovers, or workers, women often feel that other people are demanding too much of them; and they resent it. Frequently they cannot even allow themselves to admit that they resent these excess pressures. They have come to believe that they should *want* to respond at all times and in all ways.[7]

The Iron Word

Yet if a woman has intrinsic worth, sometimes it's right to form that iron word: No. Sometimes it's right to recognize that she can give no more if she is still to respect herself.

Lee came to realize that. And so did I. I've developed a safeguard for myself, a personal motives test. Before I decide to take on some new responsibility, I check to see if I'm trying to fill my own cracked and empty cistern through mis-giving. I ask myself:

☐ How would I feel if the person never acknowledged receipt of the giving—martyred? resentful?

☐ Am I secretly asking for much more in return than I'm overtly admitting?

☐ Do I *have* to give to feel important?

☐ Am I vying for that person's attention?

☐ Do I feel I must "save" the other person from some flaw within himself or herself or from some outside pressure?

If I find the answer is yes to any of those questions, either I clear up my motives or choose not to give.

Those questions always cut me to the quick and help keep me on the level of giving for the joy of giving. They enable me to use my God-given bent out of love for him, for myself, and for the other person.

Lee, too, has learned how to care for herself as well as others through some simple practices. She takes her phone off the hook when she's tired. She has reshuffled her relationships, calling the deeply needy people in her life "ministries" rather than "friends." That helps her to differentiate between the people who nurture her and the people who consistently need nurturing.

Lee also is learning how to let her hurting friends take responsibility for their own lives. She now tells her needy friends: "I can do this much to help you; beyond that, it's your responsibility." Now her friends are beginning to take positive steps to help themselves—some for the first time.

Lee allows herself to complete only two encouraging acts per workday. Maybe a phone call to someone before work and a quick note to someone during break. "It's amazing how fast you can use up your quota," she admits. "But when I finish my day, I'm no longer undone by all that I've done."

A Time to Take

Please hear me clearly. I'm not advocating such self-absorption that we refuse to extend ourselves to others. I'm saying that Lee and I are learning to love ourselves *so* we can love others. And that receiving is a healthy expression of self-love, too. Receiving, of course, needs to be balanced with the giving so we don't become permanent takers, which is an unlovely thing to become.

To find that balance requires sensitivity to God. Sometimes, in some relationships, he calls on us to receive little back—ever. Sometimes, for a period of time, he asks that in a certain relationship we assume we will only give (e.g., during a time of crisis or illness or special stress). Sometimes during our personal crises we only receive and have no resources from which to give. But relationships usually are a blend of giving and receiving.

When God moved me twice in seven months, each time to

a new state and a new job, all my initiative to be an aggressive giver wilted like warm lettuce. I was too emotionally tired, and besides, I didn't know that many people. (Though we mis-givers are great at finding the needy people in a community as soon as we move in.) But I just didn't have anything from which to give—good or bad, strength or weakness; there were no resources to draw on.

God, meanwhile, planted giving people into my life. People who cleaned my house when I was too sick to do it myself. People who filled my refrigerator just before I got back from a trip. People who listened and listened and listened when I was lonely for old friends and old locations and had to tell *someone* about my unhappiness. And all I could do was accept their gifts. For I had nothing out of which I could give to them.

Now, even after experiencing the joy of receiving and giving in healthy ways, I still fall into the habit of giving out of weakness. Just a few months ago I listened to a man talk for four hours about a book he wanted me to accept on behalf of the publishing house I worked for. I realized very shortly into our conversation that it wasn't the kind of book we could successfully sell. But he was insistent on telling me the *whole* outline of the book. "Well, he *needs* someone to listen," I rationalized. So I listened, even though it would have been better for both of us if I had given honesty instead of a listening ear.

But I *am* learning to ask myself if I'm acting out of love for the other person and for myself in giving or taking. Despite its potential abuse, I'm still convinced giving is one of the most beautiful qualities a woman has to bestow on her coworkers.

How about You?

Now it's time for you to take a look at a couple of tough situations. Think through how you would respond. It'll help you decide just how healthy your giving is.

1. It's Friday night. You're wearily walking through the front

door, thrilled to be home and thinking about soaking off the hard week in the bathtub after convincing your husband to make a run to McDonald's for dinner. You've been out several nights this week, being a good listener and helper for hurting friends. Just as your foot dangles over the tub's edge, the phone rings. Against your better judgment, you answer it. It's a friend whose dog was just hit by a car. She's distraught and can't think of what to do. What are your options? Which do you think you'd pick and why? How do you weigh your needs against your friend's?

2. You've just moved into a new community. Adjusting to your new job, finding new friends, figuring out where to buy your groceries, and finding your way on unfamiliar roads are eating up all your energies. You still have boxes to unpack, you need to find a church you enjoy and a dentist because you've developed a toothache. You've just finished reading a "Dear Jane" letter from the fellow back home. A coworker, whom you like but don't know very well, shows up and asks how she can help you. What are your options? Which option do you choose and why? What might have been her responses (both positive and negative) to the other options?

3. In giving, I'd rate myself:

Folded arms   Outstretched arms

In receiving, I'd rate myself:

Folded arms   Outstretched arms

Find a comfortable niche and a block of time to have a long talk with God about where you are as a giver and a taker and where you want to be. Take time to listen to his point of view.

CHAPTER 9

Flexibility for New Challenges

Women are the traditionalists of a society, the maintainers of the status quo." "Women are the 'nest' builders who are reluctant to move or change."

These prevalent views of women are limiting. And they ignore an important fact: Change is an integral part of a woman's life, more so than a man's.

Even as an adolescent, the male moves toward solidity in his identity while the female does not. If the boy has discovered he enjoys science and does well, he sets about to prepare for a college that offers a good program to launch him in his scientific career.

The girl, on the other hand, purposefully maintains a flexible identity that can adapt to an as-yet-unknown husband. If she forms too distinct an identity, she may position herself as unmarriageable. If, for example, she is strong in science, she is not likely to decide to become a nuclear physicist. Suppose she meets a fellow in shining armor on a white horse—who is sure he does not want to marry a female nuclear physicist?

The girl usually deems such a stake too high to even think about gambling. She'll tend to choose a more traditional job that requires less preparation and can easily be scrapped. Flexibility becomes woman's watchword:

> Woman lives by adjusting to and preparing for anticipated and unanticipated contingencies: the unknown qualities of the future husband, lack of guarantee of marriage, possible economic necessity of work, possible childlessness, children leaving home, and divorce or widowhood.[1]

The Apex of Flexibility

Flexibility comprises a female strength, along with the other qualities we've looked at, vulnerability and giving. If even one segment of a woman's life is examined—bearing and raising children—it becomes clear that flexibility is critical. As a woman goes through pregnancy, change is the rule of each day, both emotionally and physically. Her mind and body are preparing her to become a mother.

Once the baby is born, change is still the rule, for the child grows every day physically and mentally. The child needs someone there who can respond to his or her maturing. The mother, as caretaker, must adapt each day to the child's growth. What satisfied today will not satisfy tomorrow.[2]

The hardest aspect of finding so few certainties in her intimate relationships is that, as society is structured today, a woman ends up in a double bind. Regardless of what route she chooses, she'll experience conflicts in roles and a constant need to juggle responsibilities. She can choose one of three paths:[3]

1. The traditional role of marriage. This woman may well

find herself and others asking a hard question: Why didn't you accomplish more in the world of work?

2. The achievement role. This woman works to achieve in a career and bypasses marriage and family altogether. She'll be questioned—and question herself—for her unorthodox choice.

3. The bimodal role. This woman combines family and career—to varying degrees. Everyday she'll suffer from the pulls and strains of two vastly different but important arenas in her life. And she'll face the constant temptation to try to be a superwoman and "do it all."

My friends and I often mentally bounce back and forth between choices. We generally conclude that marriage alone is enticing but imprisoning. But pure career is emotionally limiting and unsatisfactory for the long-range. So then we contemplate a combination of career and marriage—and get exhausted at the prospect. What's a woman to do?!

Creating New Visions

Sad to say, no comfortable role exists for us today. It's a part of our broken femininity that is doubly difficult to deal with because its solution must be found by society as a whole and not just by individual women. But our consolation is that as we struggle to adjust to constant change we find ourselves involved in an important process.

Psychologist Jean Miller calls it *creativity*.[4] Not creativity in the sense of creating an artwork, but in breaking through to a new vision. It's finding new definitions of ourselves and new ways to see and to express our worth. It's discovering there is validity in being a wife, or a mother, or a single woman. It's seeing there is no "right" stance one can choose for life. All the options have merits and demerits; they all require a woman to consistently break through to new and positive ways of seeing herself.

"This very personal kind of creativity," Miller states, "this making of new visions, this continuous struggle, does not usually go on in open and well-articulated ways."[5] We may not realize that other women also wrestle for definitions and are unable to find fixity.

A new mother who has worked for years but decides to stay home with her baby struggles against the shocking, silent solitude of her home. Trips to the grocery store become the week's climax. How does this woman redefine herself?

A working mother watches as her sick child falls asleep at last. She glances at the clock—4 A.M.—and wonders how she'll handle her tough client appointment, just four hours away. How can she positively define herself and her multiple roles? What about the pulls and strains that tear at her from so many directions?

Part of the answer must come from the significant men in these women's lives. How can they help to authenticate these women in their shifting, pressured roles? But much of the answer also must come from within the women. We need to see that this struggle for new visions and new definitions isn't just a painful experience. It has rewards. God often calls his people to new views of themselves, to be creative and flexible in their understanding of who they are. Sometimes he helps his children to discover a vision by giving them new names. Abram, for example, was in desperate need of a new vision, when at age 99, God still hadn't given him his promised son. God visited him and renamed him the Father of Many. And Sarai became Sarah. The new names were God's urgings to break through to a new view of their potential before they saw a tangible result—their son.

Simon, the man of shifting-sand character, was renamed Peter, the Rock. His transformation was not instantaneous, but his name foreshadowed the character change and presented Peter with a creative vision of the man he could be.

No Ordinary Experience

Sometimes God doesn't bother with new names to spur people on to new visions. In Mary's case God asked her to bear his Son while she had no husband and then to have her first child in a barnyard after traveling ninety miles on a donkey. Then, for the rest of her life, she had to consistently face that being Jesus' mother was no ordinary mothering experience. Yet she displayed great flexibility and cast aside simple—and societal—definitions of her appropriate role.

In Genesis, Joseph found himself transformed from favorite son to slave in one day. Then from Potiphar's business manager to prisoner. And from prisoner to prime minister. Because God was the focal point of his life, he mustered the flexibility to accept each new role and then to move on to another one.

Paul commented on the flexibility he had acquired as he served God: "I have learned to be content whatever the circumstances. I know what it is to be in need, and I know what it is to have plenty. I have learned the secret of being content in any and every situation, whether well fed or hungry, whether living in plenty or in want. I can do everything through him who gives me strength" (Philippians 4:11-13). God deems flexibility an important part of character formation.

While everyone strives for this creativity, women have the additional challenge of finding a creative view of themselves in binding roles. The activity of creating new vision, of displaying flexibility, is an integral part of a woman's life. There are a couple of key ways in which flexibility is worked out in a woman's life. First, flexibility becomes evident as a woman chooses to care for others. For women, caring for others and participating in others' development is a major component of their self-esteem which helps them to be flexible in the middle of their binding roles.[6]

And that caring is an admirable—and godly—trait. Remember how Jesus claimed that the command to love your neighbor as yourself was one of two commands on which all the law and prophets hung? When I recall his statement, I picture two hinges on a door. The edict to love our neighbor and the edict to love God combine to open to us, like hinges, a world of warmth, challenge, pain and pleasure.

The second expression of that adaptability is being able to learn in different ways. Learning is generally thought of as the process of acquiring knowledge of how to do something or how to operate something and then applying that knowledge exactly as one learned it, or applying a principle from one situation to another.[7] I call this "fixed learning." One uses this type of learning when driving a car for the first time and then applies it to operating a tractor.

Being a caretaker of children involves a totally different and more complex kind of learning, an "adaptable learning." Miller points out that "What one learned yesterday is not good enough and does not apply today. One cannot hope to use it exactly, not even by analogy, because the situation has already changed."[8] Teaching Elizabeth to say "please" today is very different from explaining to her why she mustn't be sassy tomorrow.

Bringing Creativity to Society

Miller suggests that we can bring this concept of learning for change rather than for fixity to society and to our jobs. It's a concept that would bring refreshment and creativity.[9] She notes:

> Some societies, particularly ours, attempt to divert the need for change by entertainment, and a rapid succession of fads. All of these "circuses" may convey the illusion of change, but in fact they accomplish the opposite. They do not meet the need for growth and enlargement of the mind. Instead they often confuse us so much that we overlook the terrible frustration of this true need. They thwart rather than fulfill it.[10]

For example, as one thinks about the confusion in roles today, many people blame the feminists for setting us all on the edge of uncertainty: Who are we and how do we relate? Yet, even in the midst of the confusion, because of creative thinking, women have demanded new definitions. It's not sufficient to live with superficial change, to teach society to say "men *and women.*" But to *see* women achieve—and not just the immensely gifted ones—that's change.

In turn, men have re-examined their roles and are beginning to discover that they have passed up some valuable experiences. More men are finding out that being a father can be an excitingly active role rather than a passive one. Changing and bathing Baby is also Dad's duty. Fathering, men are realizing, begins before John III should learn how to throw a ball.

That greater male involvement in caretaker-tasks helps to alleviate woman's double-bind because it frees her to nurture herself and to discover and use more of her abilities. It frees the man to use all his abilities and to find new definitions of himself, and it offers to children a more complete and balanced family life. Women have been in the vanguard of these changing roles, to the benefit of all.

As women enter more fully into the marketplace, we have an opportunity to use our greater flexibility. As Jane Adams interviewed successful women, she found that they all advocated one important piece of advice: while following the prescribed rules for succeeding in a profession, exploit one or two traits or styles that are deemed antithetical to success.[11]

One frequently cited trait was flexibility, especially in setting goals. Dru Scott, a West Coast consultant, explained her philosophy as follows:

When you internalize a specific goal, you get locked into it. You miss seeing the other opportunities that exist, because you're always looking several steps ahead. You are not living in the present, but in the future.[12]

Most of the women advocated step-by-step goal setting. An executive woman noted, "One particular place may be a lever or a springboard, but I usually see it first for itself, as a growing and learning possibility. By coming to a corner and turning it, your goals often change." She stated that she thought men were more structured and less imaginative in their goals than women.[13]

The women specified four to ten years to accomplish their present objectives and viewed their plans afterward as highly flexible. They felt they had clarified their purposes and that was more important than setting goals.[14] So a woman may decide her purpose is to produce quality work on time while caring for her people. Or to be consistently fulfilled and growing while helping others to advance.

Flexing on the Job

The women also displayed greater flexibility in their perceptions of themselves in their jobs. Ann Howell, director of the Fort Mason Foundation in San Francisco, said,

> There is a difference between being a leader and being a manager. The staff needs a manager, but the project needs a leader—it is an ongoing conflict, with a different style required for different times and purposes. I think being able to be flexible and step into those roles as they are required is a major ingredient of my success.[15]

Each woman needs to examine her situation and see where flexibility is needed. As manager of a publications department of forty people, I found flexibility essential when people were in need of attention. Often my office door was like an overworked gumball machine, dispensing people into my office *ad infinitum.*

Sometimes I was tempted to be inflexible and to keep my pen to the paper, impatiently and hurriedly dealing with the latest interruption. But usually I kept my door ajar, because I sensed early on that flexibility was an important asset in that job. By my conviction I chose people over product. And, to be honest, I loved it! Yet my availability may have been both a strength and a weakness. I was there for people, which was good and important. Yet maybe I was too available, becoming less effective as a manager and fostering dependence among the other writers.

Helping Others to Flex

Another woman used her flexibility to help others see situations anew. Catherine was asked to serve on her church's Committee on the Use of Women's Gifts. The committee members had mixed opinions. Some were supportive of new roles for women. Others wondered what the fuss was about. They asked, "There are enough things for the women to do. Why do they want more? What's going to happen to the men if the women become leaders?"

Catherine responded by suggesting flexibility: "Why not have the men teach the junior-high girls' group? The girls who are from broken homes need to be with men; it would be a special ministry only a man could have.

"And think about when we dedicate babies. We covenant as a congregation to pray for them. How can the men pray for them when they don't know them? Why not have men work in the nursery?"

Well, the suggestions may have been well reasoned, but the committee members weren't ready for them. Yet Catherine's flexible thinking opened up the committee to new options they might not have considered otherwise.

The word *flexibility*, you'll note, keeps rising to the surface like a buoy among the waves—flexibility in goals, direction, orientation, methods, view of self. But how does all this translate into reality? How can we nurture our womanly flexibility? Here are a few steps:

1. Become more aware of how you express that quality. For a week, at the end of each day, make a list of ways you were flexible. What situations were easy to flex in? Which were hard? Why?

2. Use creative learning on the job. Think through areas where creative learning could be effectively applied. Where, for example, does the situation change from day to day? What systems seem to consistently stymie coworkers? How could you implement or suggest change? How could you help coworkers to flex in the changing circumstances?

3. Look for personal ways to display flexibility at work. Ask yourself, "If this were a family, what would a mother do?" The answer usually falls into one of these categories:

She'd—be quick to listen
    —attempt to rescue
    —respond graciously
    —find creative and stimulating solutions
    —make the best of a hard situation.

Note: This exercise is *not* to make you the "mother" at work; it's to help you express your flexibility in the work environment. And since women have most highly developed their flexibility in dealing with children, it's a likely place to look to learn principles.

4. Watch women as they fulfill everyday duties of grocery shopping, caring for children, laundering, cooking. How do they display flexibility? How can that be translated into your profession?

5. Write your purpose statement. Make it one sentence that states what you want to achieve either in life or in your present job. It may center around acquisition of skills or professional growth. You could also include what you intend to *give* to coworkers and to the company.

In many ways, the issue of how effectively a woman leads returns to her self-perception. Will you display your flexible nature? Will you bring an aura of changeability and creativity? Or will you respond in prescribed ways? You *are* capable of being a change-agent in society. Such a role affirms your adaptability. The choice is yours.

CHAPTER 10

A Cooperative Nature

The idea is unorthodox. Carolyn, who is assistant director of surgery for twenty-four operating rooms, involves the nurses in their overall direction. The nurses set aside one hour each day to work toward meeting the goals of the entire department.

Carolyn is utilizing one of women's strengths, cooperation. She understands that a team spirit, a sense of the group working toward a common good with mutual benefit for all, can bring out positive traits in everyone, *especially women*.

If we break down the word *cooperation*, we understand it more fully. *Co* signifies "with." We are "with" others rather than standing independently. *Operate* comes from a Latin word meaning "to work." When we cooperate, we work with others for mutual benefit.

Patients as People

Carolyn discovered just how beneficial cooperation is when the nurses began to see the results of their labors. One of the programs they instituted was visiting patients before and after surgery. They explained to the patient how the operating room functioned and what the patient would experience. "The nurses wanted to be part of that experience for the patient," Carolyn said, "rather than just dealing with the patient as a body.

"We did an effectiveness study to convince management that this idea paid off. We found we were reducing hospital stays by one day. That amounts to thousands of dollars saved by a hospital our size." Not to mention the added motivation for the nurses, and the patient's sense of being well cared-for.

Creating such a mutually beneficial program is a natural outgrowth of how women successfully function as leaders. Studies show that women tend to cooperate while men compete; women are more trusting than men; women more often voluntarily give their opponents a larger share of available resources than do men; they are less likely to make an initial offer that is favorable to themselves, and more likely to make a final offer that provides the other with the larger share of the resource. Men play to win; women play to avoid losing. As one researcher concluded, "Females adopt an anti-competitive strategy in bargaining situations, seeming more interested in obtaining fair outcomes than in winning, while males seek only victory."[1]

Of course, the problem with women expressing cooperation—working to enhance others *and* themselves—is that it's not a generally accepted pattern of leadership. A "male" view of leadership was presented to me during a break in a meeting one day.

"Intelligence and competition are connected," Kevin pontificated as he twirled his empty styrofoam cup in his hands. "If you are truly intelligent and a good leader, you'll also be a strong competitor on the athletic field."

I didn't know how to respond. I'm not athletic in mind or body! My TV doesn't even know how to sniff out a sports program, and my body simply wasn't designed to interact with sports equipment. The only game I'm competitive in is Scrabble. But, I don't view myself as unintelligent or as an incompetent leader.

"Kevin, how did you reach that conclusion?" I finally asked. Kevin had observed male leaders and decided that each melded brains with a brawny competitive spirit. So, he decided, all leaders must have these qualities.

To Compete or Not to Compete

Fifty managerial women were asked to rate their competitive behavior in their organizations. Out of the fifty women, more than twenty-five stipulated neutrality with both men and women peers. Only twelve of the women saw themselves as slightly competitive, and of those twelve, four indicated that they were more competitive with women than with men.[2]

Those who saw themselves as competitive felt they had a healthier view than a me vs. you attitude. One woman stated, "I always compete for the marketplace, not against another specific individual. . . . I don't like the win/lose model, and I think it's a poor use of energy."[3]

One woman, who is a sales rep for a large printing firm, says, "I avoid an adversarial posture at all costs with the people I work with, especially men. My goal is to establish a relationship of benefit. I want the other person to see how I can benefit him or how it's to his benefit to help me. That kind of philosophy makes my working relationships really pleasant."

The women saw themselves as leaders who didn't need to compete. They had discovered other successful ways to operate. They expressed teamwork by offering to form triple coalitions when two-person coalitions would suffice; dividing prizes equally instead of according to bargaining strength; offering to form a coalition to their own disadvantage.

Sometimes it doesn't have to be some big, grandiose move that makes the difference. Something simple can help move a group into a team mindset. Even a few well-chosen words, coupled with a relaxed tone of voice, can make a big difference. "Can you help me to understand the main objection you have to the proposal?" "What facts caused you to decide against the motion?" "Is there a third option we haven't even thought of?" These responses can throw open the windows to let fresh air in on a stale debate and can help people examine their rigid positions.

Big bargaining moves and little words intended to change a mind are two methods a person can use to modify the more exploitative strategy that's often seen in organizations. The main point is that cooperation directs a leader's energies to advance as many people as possible.

One leader who instilled a team spirit into a group was Jesus. In Luke 9 he heard his rag-tag "team" arguing about who deserved top-dog position (vv. 46-48). In response Jesus took a small child to them, placed his arm on the child's shoulder and looked at his disciples.

"To welcome this child is to welcome me," Jesus said. "And to welcome me is to welcome my Father."

"Now, what does *that* mean?" the disciples may well have wondered as they frowned at the child.

Then Jesus brought his point home: "To be the greatest one in this group, you have to be the least."

He Who Stoops Low

Sometimes Jesus stooped low to show the disciples that they must also. Like when he washed their feet (John 13:5-17). They didn't understand, and Peter protested that this uncomfortable behavior wasn't in conformity with Jesus' job description.

When Jesus had finished wiping off the last drop of water, he tossed the towel over his shoulder and said, "Do you understand what I've just done?"

Of course they did—he'd just washed their feet like a servant would. Of course they didn't—they knew it meant something more.

"You have shown me respect," he said, "and that is appropriate. But I have just given you an example. I want you to remember you should stoop down and serve each other out of mutual care. Promote one another. Be for each other."

Again the disciples saw that being part of a team wasn't an easy thing. But their leader had shown them how beautiful this hard thing was. And I suspect their hearts hungered to care for one another in this way.

My favorite scene of Jesus calling his people to cooperate with each other is one of his last. The disciples were out fishing after Jesus' crucifixion, wondering what to do with all the lessons that made their hearts burn in longing to live them out.

Jesus called to them from the shore, and when they realized who he was they worked like mad to get to shore quickly so they could see their leader, their friend, their living God. He was crouching over a fire, poking at the quietly sizzling fish. His robe was full of the smell of smoke and breakfast. How like him. No pious posturing. No demanding an exalted position. Even in a moment of great drama, he was frying a few fish for them. He was reminding them to cooperate and care for each other.

The Balancing Act

Cooperation is an essential element in building a team. But like the other characteristics we have looked at, it can be misused in addition to well-used. Cooperation can go wrong when a woman consistently denies her own needs to meet the needs of others. Women sometimes have difficulty supporting others' interests along with their own. Many women struggle with even the possibility of wanting something for themselves.[4]

One sociologist observed an example of this at a convention. A man engaged a woman friend in conversation. He dominated the discussion by listing his year's achievements: research notes, book reviews, monographs, projects, and on and on. The woman only listened.[5] By accepting his dominance of the conversation and receiving all that he said, she was making him feel good while she appeared passive. She was deprecating herself by allowing dominance of her person; she became *subservient* rather than *supportive* and raised his status by lowering her own.

The dividing line between supportive (which can be a positive expression of teamwork) and subservient comes when the one person is *always* of prime importance and the other individual is *always* passive. It's no longer a matter of who is "first," to talk or to receive attention, but that there is no "second." The person who always accepts being the other's ego booster has not expressed self-love.

This kind of behavior is more likely to occur when you interact with your supervisor or with peers. But it can crop up, too, when you deal with subordinates. You can be busy expressing interest in them and thinking you're being a servant when in actuality the relationship is one-sided.

I tend to fall into this pit sometimes. This was especially true when I worked with male peers who all possessed powerful personalities, all knew what they wanted to accomplish, and all had plans for how I could help them accomplish it.

My first warning sign that I have fallen into the pit again is when I discover that I'm feeling depersonalized and used. Guess whose fault that is?! At that point, I try to force myself to volunteer information to make our conversations less one-sided: "That seminar was a super experience because . . . ." "Did I tell you about my weekend yet . . . ?" "I'm concerned about the meeting we just attended." I am assuming that the other person wants to take a turn in listening and receiving. It forces me to re-establish myself as an important person in my own eyes as well as someone else's.

Then I look for opportunities for more in-depth interaction: "Were you aware that you seemed disinterested in others when you . . . ?" "It might be helpful for you to know that your second point seemed a bit unclear . . ." "Could you look over something I wrote and give me your opinion?" That moves the relationship into mutuality, which makes it more stimulating for both parties.

Stuck on a Star

Working as a team can lead to another abuse of woman's strength. A woman can "hide out" in the group and not take individual risks. Because she sees risk differently from men, this can be a tempting way to let a strength become a weakness. Men see risk as loss or gain; winning or losing; danger or opportunity. Women view risk as negative. Words such as *loss, danger, injury, ruin* and *hurt* define *risk* to women.[6]

Men perceive risk as affecting the future; women see it as ruining the here and now. One woman explained the difference graphically: "My husband always says to me, 'Shoot for the moon and the worst you can do is fall on a star!' And I've just realized that every time he says it I always respond, 'Sure you will. On one of the points.' "[7]

Because women tend to view risk as loss and failure, they find it harder to be aggressive and to gamble. It is easier to play it safe, to hide in a group, and to hope someone will notice you do good work and push you on in your career.

Part of the hesitancy to risk is wrapped up in women's lack of confidence. In one study, men and women took a test and then indicated how well they thought they did. The women underrated their performances; the men overrated theirs.[8] That makes it clearer why women hesitate to take on a risk or a challenging task while men leap in where women fear to tread.

Obviously we must strike a balance between taking risks to advance ourselves and working to create a strong sense of team. Competition alone can create a politically heated atmosphere and an excessive absorption in work. But if cooperation is developed, there's a greater emphasis on solidarity, an awareness of helping others, and a sense that success has many definitions. It's that spirit of cooperation that women can bring to an organization to complement more competitive men. Both sides end up winning.

Application Time

1. Look over next month's calendar. What situations are coming up in which cooperation could be an important quality to display (for example, a budget meeting, a planning session, a hard phone call, a confrontation you need to make)? Write out specific ways you can create a team spirit.

2. If risk were a color, what color would it be? Why?

3. When was the last time you took a risk? What good came from the experience? What bad? Talk that experience over with God. Tell him how you feel about it. Then ask him for his perspective on it.

4. Ask God if you need to say yes to some risk in your life. Plan, with him, a specific time and strategy to begin.

CHAPTER 11

Close Connections

The woman sat in my office, sniffling, wadding up Kleenex after Kleenex as she tried to explain why she was so distraught. The project I'd given her had developed into a behemoth, much to our amazement. The woman had done her best despite the added complications of a broken engagement and her father's sudden death. She needed to be released from the project. I reassigned the job to a person with more writing experience and less stress in his personal life.

In some ways the decision seems obvious. Compassion was an important criterion. But in management, compassion is somewhat rare. Here again a central characteristic of women can enhance the rosy bloom in an organization's cheeks. As women, we've been given the task of developing and caring for others as our major work; in many ways that function naturally carries over to our leadership roles. Dr. Jean Miller states, "Women have a much greater sense of the pleasures of close connection with physical, emotional, and mental growth than men."[1]

A People Person

Psychologist Esther Harding remarks on the importance of people in a woman's work:

> There is a certain kind of impersonality which kills a woman's interest. If her work is purely mechanical, such as filing index cards, or moving a lever to and fro on a machine, her interest is, as a rule, not satisfied, as a man's perhaps might be, in working out a new system, or in discovering *how* it is done, or even in coming to love the machine. She will either become a sort of robot or she will turn away from the task and occupy herself with the person for whom she is doing it.[2]

For a man, freedom is autonomy; a woman feels free and fulfilled in successful relationships. But everyone—men and women—develop personally through affiliation; being closely connected to others is *the* means for personal growth.[3] Think about what such a trait could do to enhance an organization if more leaders expressed it.

Jesus modeled this characteristic for us when in Matthew 12:1-14 he debated with the Pharisees about which was more important: the sabbath or a person. In this passage, the question came up first when the disciples plucked some grain and hungrily chomped on it while they walked through a field.

The Pharisees gasped and pointed their fingers at such affrontery. Jesus responded by calmly giving the Pharisees a history lesson on David and his cohorts eating the consecrated bread. He was trying to give the Pharisees a bit of perspective on life by reminding them that God gives gold stars to those who express mercy, not just religiously follow rule books.

They weren't favorably impressed with the lesson, as shown by the next scene in this passage. Jesus goes to the synagogue. There he finds a man with a shriveled, nut-brown hand. The Pharisees taunt Jesus by asking him what his stand is regarding sabbath healings. Once again Jesus reaffirms the priority of people over the calendar and heals the man.

The Pharisees gasp and point—but this time they end up whispering murderous thoughts to each other about Jesus. Jesus, as God's physical expression, made it clear that connecting with people with a spirit of mercy is the route God favors.

Friendly Affirmation

As a woman proceeds in her career, she'll find her subordinates respond well to her affirmation of the value of people. Studies show that "on the job, women were rewarded more for administering in a person-oriented manner."[4]

In one study, three supervisory styles (directive, rational and friendly) were portrayed by men and women supervisors. They, in turn, were rated by thirty men and women nonmanagers. The preferred style for any manager was the emotional, friendly approach, followed by the rational. The directive, authoritarian style was the least favorite. The authoritarian style was especially disliked by men when it was displayed by women managers.[5]

The friendly leadership style comes naturally for women in our culture. Studies report that even as children, females are more socially oriented than males, regardless of age.

Girls are more concerned about the welfare of other children, they play more social games, they are more interested in books about people, they are more interested in occupations dealing with people, they are more concerned about appearance and manners, they ask more questions about social relations, and they are more often jealous.[6]

A woman's social nature is shown in that she is also better able to express affection than men, both with members of the same and the opposite sex.[7]

Psychologist Martin Hoffman found that females are more empathetic than males. Even in studies of newborn babies, girls are more likely to cry in response to a tape recording of another infant crying. The empathetic difference between males and females is found consistently, regardless of the age of those tested.[8]

The Fly in the Ointment

But this quality, like the others, can be abused and expressed as a weakness. Women view affiliation so highly that psychologists say they place greater value on relationships than on self-enhancement. And some women find having a significant other in their lives so important that everything else becomes meaningless.

A counselor tells of one patient, Barbara, who holds a high academic appointment. She's a "rigorous and independent thinker," but she also feels empty and worthless because there is no man in her life.[9]

Beatrice, a successful businesswoman who could "persuade shrewd bargainers who intimidated many men," would say, "What does it all mean if there isn't a man who cares about me?"[10]

This distorted aspect of the need for affiliation causes a woman tremendous conflict. And it affects her attitude at work. Her view of herself as a competent, worthwhile person can falter because of the lack of a significant other. Her career motivation can stumble and fall if she diverts her attention to finding a man. Because it so intensely affects other angles of our lives, we need to explore the personal side of this weakness in depth.

Developing a close tie with a man can become so important to a woman that she becomes subservient. The seeds of such behavior are apparent even in children.

Girls develop a tendency to react to others rather than acting as individuals. Thus their behavior becomes "tuned" to what others expect, and their concern with understanding the needs and motives of others—especially males—is greater. This is particularly evident in adolescence, when girls are more concerned with understanding boys than with understanding themselves.[11]

Beatrice, the successful businesswoman, for example, worked to tightly bind a particular man to her. She wasn't a passive, dependent woman, but all of her activity was directed to the binding of this man. Her counselor pointed out that Beatrice didn't really need that kind of relationship—but Beatrice wasn't convinced of it.[12]

The problem generated a great deal of unexpected anger for Beatrice. When the man she was attempting to manipulate didn't cooperate, she became furious. How else could she respond when she had given so much control of her life to another?[13] She was convinced she *had* to have him tightly embraced in her life; when he refused, she saw no other option but misery and anger.

Miller suggests that women must face certain frightening questions about what cements them to their manipulative behavior with a significant other: If I admit that I can direct my own life rather than letting others do it, can I exist with safety? with satisfaction? Who will ever love me, or even tolerate me, if I am so independent?[14]

Winning over Manipulation

A woman must stare down these issues and finally determine that out of self-respect and fairness to others she must break her manipulative pattern. It may take her years to come to this conclusion, but if she is going to develop her abilities and enjoy herself, she must.

I know from personal experience how long and painful we

can make this process for ourselves. One of my friends once described me as "a woman who knows what she wants and goes after it." Independent. Strong. Determined. Stubborn. Unfortunately, I expressed my determination wrongly and manipulated any man I wanted bound into my life.

The crowning example of how destructive that can be came when I met Curt, a man who more than matched my white-knight expectations: brilliant, handsome, cultured, athletic; an academician, a scholar, an actor, a musician, a writer, a poet, a gourmet cook. I even loved his personal library of two thousand books in four languages, many of them first editions from the eighteenth and nineteenth centuries.

But, unfortunately, Curt projected the most awesome personality I'd ever encountered. I was out of my league when it came to strength and independence. Manipulation didn't move him—either closer to me or farther away. He had decided just where he stood in relation to me and had struck an immovable pose. After years of frustration, I decided to try to manipulate Curt through acquiescence rather than direct action. Rather than tie him to me, I'd tie myself to him. Rather than convince him he needed me, I'd expend every energy to please him. His approval became paramount—even over God's.

God, of course, being a jealous God, insisted on an immediate reordering of relational importance. He *would* be first. I refused to reorder priorities.

So I could not be surprised when the relationship with Curt ended and I was devastated. I had believed I could be happy only if I had Curt. Now what would I do? I was like the crystal Christmas ornament I once dropped in a store. The gossamer-thin glass shattered into so many pieces it looked like a pile of powdered snow on the oak floor.

Through that shattering I reinstated God as the prime person in my life and I asked myself some hard questions: Can I safely determine my own direction in life and not choose to merely respond to others? Can I be satisfied without a man? Can I be happy and whole without a man? Will anyone ever love me? Am I unlovable?

The questions propelled me into God's arms: He loved me despite my fickleness. He cared enough not to let me manipulate this man deeper into a flawed relationship that would only have caused more destruction to us both. He wanted to help me love and respect myself enough never to acquiesce to another person out of desperation. He wanted to make my future beautiful, not binding.

Looking back, with many years in between, I'm speechless with gratitude that God didn't allow me to bind Curt to me. I know now that I would have felt so crushed by the pressure of trying to be anything to please a man that eventually I would have burned Curt's library as a statement that deep inside, a strong person wanted *out*.

Those lessons have been repeated over the years as I have forgotten them and made the same mistake with other men. But I've learned a lot: vulnerability and honesty are paramount in any primary relationship; to be anything less than I know myself capable of is to lack self-love; a relationship should free me to be more, not bind me to be less; no relationship can make me happy; happiness comes from within me.

Discovering the "More" in Life

I discovered that once I decided to live by these principles, a basic question rose to the surface: What do I really want? Only as a person grapples with this question does she begin to see how to attain satisfaction. As she grapples, she realizes that fulfillment really is possible. And fulfillment doesn't come from outside, but from within.

She doesn't *really* want the binding she thought she did.[15] She wants mutuality and respect. And if she's a strong woman, one other aspect is prime to her in a relationship: independence.

Jane Adams found an intense need for independence—in every phase of adulthood—in the managerial women she interviewed.[16] Many of the women who married in their early twenties at first acquiesced to cultural cues to limit their independence. But independence became the central issue of their divorces, if and when they occurred, or of the realignment of power in their marriages.[17]

As young women, they also gave long and careful consideration to becoming mothers, asking themselves just how much a child would impede their personal independence. A successful executive woman saw her marriage this way:

"The way you start is the way you end up." My mother told me that, and she was right. Our marriage has worked because it was clear from the beginning that my career was as important to me as his was to him. It has not always worked out in actual fact—my role as wife and mother is an additional one. I could have them both and pursue my career, knowing that he could fill in for me if it was absolutely essential.[18]

One woman determined to remain single, saying:

I can survive if I don't [marry]. And furthermore, I told myself, I'm going to work terribly hard at making sure it's more than survival and make it really awfully good. With the friends, the theater dates, Chinese food ordered in for eight couples on a Saturday night even if I don't have a man to be the host. It didn't matter; I just wanted my home, my life, friendships, traveling, my career, and gee, I wish I were married but so what, I will build a rich, rewarding life, full of good things, full of satisfactions, and with independence and achievement as my goals in all of those satisfactions.[19]

As age began to limit childbearing potential, women once again evaluated their lives if they had not married or had not become mothers. For these successful women, the prime issue in reevaluating was independence. One woman said: "This was the stage at which I began to think about what I would have to give up for marriage and children, rather than what I would gain." She decided to keep on in her career and changed companies to find more satisfaction in her job.[20]

Then, after reassessing her life at midcareer, the typical successful woman enters into a period of integration. The central issue is still independence but the focus is on establishing a balance between responsibilities and rewards. In other words, deciding how high a price she would pay and what she would get for that price. At this point, women decided whether they would go for the top in their organizations or not.

The women interviewed by Adams realized that attempting to attach themselves to a man as the *major* goal in life was bondage. They realized the importance of being independent enough to use their skills and talents and to develop themselves. They viewed independence as so important they would forego much to maintain it.

Realistic Views

The woman who furtively seeks a significant other must recognize that she creates her own bondage to a vision of what she thinks that relationship will be. If she could indeed enact the relationship she has fantasized, she would discover that it's binding beyond her ability to happily bear it. Especially if she contains the strength necessary to be a good leader, independence is a treasure she can't forego as easily as she may think.

If she desires to have a significant other in her life—and seems to have a realistic view of what it would cost her—God still may choose not to give such an opportunity. Then it becomes her responsibility to live her life singly to the fullest. Her challenge is to develop herself and those in her life to their maximum. The work setting and friendships are the arenas to which she is sent to use her skills.

While there will be times that such an appointment seems hollow, lacking in sufficient dignity or happiness to satisfy, she must proceed on one unfailing fact: God is love and has acted in love toward her. She may not understand that, she may long to thwart it, but ultimately, if she is to walk with God, she must accept his expression of love to her—a career of building herself and others.

Women struggle with these independence issues as they go through each stage of life—the easy attachments of the twenties, the reassessment at the end of the thirties, and the integration of midlife. The answers never seem easy. It may be of at least small comfort to know she goes not alone—other women are with her.

With each choice something is given up but something else flowers that could not otherwise even be planted. If one bypasses marriage, greater energy can be expended on the job and in creating strong friendships. New fulfillment and opportunities to serve might blossom. If motherhood does not come, marriage might flower all the more.

The outcomes for each choice are known only in part. All we do know is that each decision contains the seed of both loss and gain. It's never all loss and all gain; the two are a package deal. Sometimes it helps me to think of life as a bag of mixed nuts. The cashews and pistachios are delights. But the peanuts, with their skins peeling off, are less savory. Overall, the taste is pleasing; but life always hands us a mixed bag of good and bad, never all of one kind.

Coping with Conflict

While the woman's desire for close relationships can get her in romantic difficulties, it can also make it hard for her to deal with conflict. Evelyn, for example, supervises eight teachers in a church-run, urban school in Detroit. The former assistant principal was a man who managed the teachers with an aloof, uncommunicative style. Morale was always low because the teachers were not well paid, and he rarely showed them appreciation.

Since Evelyn took over, the atmosphere at the school has changed dramatically. The pay scale is still low, but the teachers feel affirmed by their warm, open boss. They have become a close team. Her style of leadership is quite different from her predecessor's. But Evelyn has trouble explaining this to the principal. He thinks that she's too close to the teachers and will not be able to discipline one of them if the need arises. Evelyn is doing things in a new way, and she's not sure what to do about the principal's unenthusiastic response.

Evelyn's situation exemplifies an important principle: Anytime someone tries to do something new, conflict will arise. Conflict is an inevitable accompaniment to change. Psychologists find that to institute change a person *must* initiate conflict. This external conflict shouldn't be avoided. Out of conflict can come new knowledge of oneself, new perspectives and new actions. Conflict can bring about important beginnings. As women we tend to fear conflict because we think it brings endings rather than beginnings. In productive conflict,[21] each person involved will change his or her goals because of the interaction. They will make progress toward one another. Dr. Miller believes:

> Ideally, the new intent and goals will be larger and richer each time, rather than more restricted and cramped. That is, each party should perceive more, and want *more* as a result of each engagement and have more resources with which to act.[22]

Conflict, when productive, results in a feeling of change, expansion and joy, even though the process can involve anguish and pain.

But destructive conflict also exists.[23] It creates blocks rather than opens new ways. A person senses that he or she can't win, that nothing will change or improve because of the confrontation. One has a dread knowledge that he or she must relinquish deeply felt motives and lose connections with the most cherished desires and deeply felt needs.[24]

Despite the potential for difficulties, it's best to be open about feelings when conflict is present but has never been discussed. Miller suggests that if you *feel* conflict, you should *be* in conflict.[25] Initiate discussing your thoughts and feelings. Let the other party know that you are experiencing turmoil.

One of the greatest hindrances to confrontation is your fear of being condemned or isolated, of risking an important relationship. At this point you need to turn to others for support. They can reflect your thinking back to you so you can see if it is distorted, if you have exaggerated the situation, or if it is appropriate for you to ask for change. They can help you understand where emotion begins and logic ends. They can affirm your decision to speak up, and they can uphold you after you've done so. Just make sure your search for support is not an excuse for gossiping.

To confront takes courage. But to remain silent is to destroy relationships, your belief in yourself, and ultimately yourself. Frequently broader vistas are found only through honest confrontation.

It helps me to speak up when I realize that it's normal to want to draw others to me rather than push them away by saying unpleasant things. But actually my desire for closeness should provide me with the impetus to say those hard words. A good conflict may bring greater intimacy while a silence will destroy trust and honesty.

How To

All of which sounds glorious, but what if you just aren't natural at handling conflict? What do you do? Here are some methods you can use to help get discussions going if you need to express negative feelings or if you find yourself an arbitrator between conflicting peers or subordinates.[26]

Mediating

1. Assure both parties that they will get to express their side of the story without interruption.

2. Let one person explain the problem as he or she sees it and what has caused the conflict.

3. Let the second person state the problem and details of the conflict.

4. Restate the problem as you understand it. Help both parties to think of solutions. Ask them to choose one to act on.

5. If they can't think of one to even try, offer some yourself or have them each think about it and later submit possible solutions in writing. Then let them choose.

6. If the chosen solution doesn't work, have them choose another.

Storytelling

This method worked well for Nathan when he confronted David about his sin with Bathsheba (see 2 Samuel 12:1-10). It's a good method when *you* feel conflict but the other person doesn't recognize it. You simply relate the problem in a story format.

I did this once after I had worked on a project for a year and then was told I was doing it wrong. My supervisor looked it over and said I had done it in the wrong format—I hadn't been informed about the correct one. I would have to redo the whole thing. Distraught but unable to adequately express my frustration, I went back to my office and wrote a story about a runner and put it in my supervisor's box. It went like this:

The runner trained hard for a big race, went out there, cleared all the hurdles and breathlessly crossed the finish line in first place. Then an embarrassed judge bustled over to him and instead of placing a trophy in the runner's arms explained that the racer had violated the rules and could not be declared the winner. Flustered, the racer claimed no knowledge of these rules. "Well," the judge said, "maybe we could run the race again."

Since my supervisor had been a runner in college, he could relate to the racer's frustration. He saw how absurd it would be to try to psychologically gear up to immediately repeat a race that had just been won. And he saw the connection between my situation and the story. I still had to redo the project, but I just had to redo the major parts. It was still an arduous task, but at least it seemed do-able.

If you can't think of how to start a story, a few simple words may help: "Suppose someone . . ." or "How would you feel if someone . . ." This method brings a new view to an old situation for the other person.

Fight Form

Writing about a problem helps to defuse anger and to make each person more rational. Have both parties write out answers to these questions and then meet to talk it out:

1. Who are you in conflict with?
2. What is the problem?
3. Give two reasons for the conflict.
4. How have you tried to resolve it?
5. What are three other solutions you might try?
6. Is there anything you would like to say to the other person?

Negotiating

This method works well with an uncooperative subordinate who is not fulfilling job responsibilities.

1. State the problem as you see it, outlining the facts but not assigning blame.
2. State what you want and why. Have the subordinate do the same.
3. State what the limits are and what can't be negotiated. Offer several points you are willing to trade off. Have the subordinate say what he or she is willing to trade off.
4. Work out a mutually satisfactory agreement.

Log List and Please List

This approach puts the conflict in perspective.

1. Recognize your own imperfections by taking a hard look at the "log" in your eye. Make a list of the things you've done wrong in the relationship. How have you failed as a subordinate . . . as a supervisor? Ask God and, if appropriate, the other person to forgive you for those failings.

2. Make two "please" lists. The first, what you could do to please the other party. The second, what the other person could do to please you.

3. Decide on at least one thing you will do for the other person; set a time and place to ask the person to do one thing for you.

Conflict is, in many ways, the Waterloo for a woman as she decides how she will utilize her strengths. She can choose to let her desire for close relationships become a weakness by always trying to please others. Or she can choose to be honest. Closeness can bind a woman too tightly to others, or it can free her up to create affirming relationships.

Making It Personal

Pick a conflict you or some individuals who report to you are experiencing. Look over the list of methods to handle conflict and choose the one that seems to best suit your situation. Decide how you will adapt it to the conflict. Pick a time and a place that seems nonthreatening. It can help just to place chairs beside each other in your office rather than having a chair on either side of the desk.

Before the meeting, pray and ask God to give you a spirit of calm and a willing and able heart to hear the other side. Above all, remember that conflict can be an important growth stimulant for everyone.

CHAPTER 12

Finding
a Role
Model

I *have always wanted to be a suc-*
cess," said an executive woman. "But when I looked around,
the only image I had was the hard-bitten career woman who
sacrificed everything to her job. . . . The career women I knew
were all very one-dimensional people, and they never
laughed."[1] That executive is decrying a typical problem among
women today—the lack of positive role models.

We have looked at conflicts women face in the workplace,
and we have examined the qualities women can exercise as
strengths. In this chapter I want to explore the whole issue of
role models and our need for them. Then in the final chapter,
we will ponder power and how a woman as leader can use it
to boost her subordinates as well as herself.

The Numbers Tell the Tale

The executive woman quoted here vocalizes the problem: The choices for female role models seem to fall into two categories. Neither carries special appeal to a woman who wants responsibility yet wants to be womanly.

There's the "traditional" woman, who is loving, warm, soft, genteel and emotional. She makes a great chocolate chip cookie for her husband and can keep the cats apart while braiding Cindy's hair. But that's just it—her interests are focused on her husband and her children. She is not, at least for the time being, interested in an occupation outside the home.

The other sort of woman is unruffled both in dress and demeanor. Her starched-linen approach to life puts people off. She may be successful at what she does. She may have managed to reach a position previously held only by men. But she has done it at the expense of her humanity. She made it to the top unwrinkled, but not intact as a woman.

Such limited models exist because, to begin with, few women manage to make it to the top. Even though the statistics are full of good news for women, we still have a long way to go. On the one hand, from 1960 to 1982 women managers in America increased by more than three million—a seventy-five per cent increase in twelve years.[2] And, in 1985, women held more than thirty-three per cent of the executive, administrative and managerial positions in America. On the other hand, the so-called pink-collar clerical jobs in 1985 were held by almost eighty per cent women.[3] As Janet Giele states,

Disproportionate numbers of women are found in subordinate ranks, and large numbers of men in the high ranks. This is true in virtually every occupation and industry. Women are the school teachers in the lower grades; men are the principals and superintendents. Nurses and health care paraprofessionals are largely women; most doctors are men. The full professors at the large universities are men; many more women are in the nontenured or peripheral ranks or in the small liberal arts colleges. While women make up 20 percent of all labor union membership, they comprise only 4.7 percent of the union leadership.[4]

In the Christian arena in 1974, ninety-two per cent of the positions on the boards of Christian organizations were filled by men, and more than eighty-three per cent of the managers of such organizations were male.[5]

Along with the slim statistical representation of women goes the confusion over women's roles once they attain leadership. One researcher summarized much of society's view of women leaders this way: "If they are normal women, they are abnormal people, while if they are normal people with ordinary technical interest and capabilities, they are abnormal women. They can't be both."[6] So the woman struggles with seemingly disparate demands of sex role and work role. If she succeeds at work, she is viewed as less successful as a woman.

In a study of women lawyers, some male lawyers complained that women attorneys won cases by using feminine "wiles." Other women lawyers were informed that because they didn't use such wiles they were masculine.[7] The study points out another complication—the man's view of women leaders. Most men show reluctance to place women in positions of power.

The Men Have It

Men are reluctant for good reasons. People like homogeneity. Our tendency is to promote others of our own kind because we are comfortable with them. Like begets like. So men will tend to hire and promote other men. It's a natural human trait which must be consciously worked on to be overcome.

Add women to any group of men and the communication process immediately becomes complex because men and women have learned to relate on a sex-role basis. Men make comments such as: "They're hard to understand"; "I'm always making assumptions that turn out to be wrong." Even though some admit that the communication complexities are largely their own problem, their stated opinions reflect their desire to keep the environment comfortable by keeping women out.[8]

The informal system of relationships that makes up most organizations also encourages fencing women out. As Hennig and Jardim point out regarding an organization, "Its forms, its rules of behavior, its style of communication and its mode of relationships grow directly out of the male development experience. . . . The informal system is truly a bastion of the male life-style."[9]

Even for the men who are in favor of advancing women, pragmatism often entices them not to attempt it. They know they'll have to endure raised eyebrows, glares, silences and queries punctuated with innuendos. Margaret Mead notes,

> Once a complex activity is defined as belonging to one sex, the entrance of the other sex into it is made difficult and compromising. . . . Painting in Bali has been a male art. When a gifted little adolescent girl in the village of Batoen, where there were already sixty young men experimenting with the modern innovation of painting on paper, tried a new way of painting—by setting down what she saw rather than painting conventional stylized representations of the world—the boy artists derided and discouraged her until she gave up and made poor imitations of their style. The very difference in sex that made it possible for her to see a little differently, and so make an innovation, also made her so vulnerable that her innovation could be destroyed.[10]

So it is in leadership positions that, with the barriers of women's confusion, men's reluctance and the very maleness of the system, role models for women are scarce. Yet women long for those models, yearning for someone to help them establish themselves as individuals in a very male environment.

The solution at the moment seems to lie in two areas: first, to recognize that women who strive for leadership positions have generally already been influenced by their parents and others who were role models; and second, to explore the area of mentoring and how it can benefit the managerial woman.

Many Influences

As we've noted throughout this book, women need to view themselves creatively to see that the necessary elements—and more—already exist in their lives to make them firm, effective leaders. The same creative view reveals that women already have models to challenge and encourage them.

This was seen in a study among college women, who usually fell into two career categories: the career salient, who were motivated to have both marriage and a career; and the non-career salient. The noncareer women had mothers active in leisure pursuits. These college women felt that family or peers had had the greatest influence on them in pursuing their future plans.

Meanwhile, the career-oriented women were exposed to occupational choices of male peers, had working mothers, and had a greater background of work experience themselves. They felt influenced by faculty members and occupational role models in choosing their occupations. Both groups expressed parental approval for and encouragement of their postgraduate plans.[11]

Other studies indicate that women oriented toward careers tend to have had female faculty. As one researcher concludes from this observation, "The more role models one has for a particular behavior, the more one would think the behavior appropriate and would tend to take on those behaviors."[12]

A further study found that a "substantial category of female PhD's . . . [were] comprised of the daughters of professional women. . . . The daughters of working mothers seem more inclined to pursue definite career patterns than other women are."[13] And yet another study indicated that these women had mothers who often worked in male-dominated professions.[14]

Surprisingly, tests suggest that fathers don't play key roles in career decisions for their daughters. But once that decision is made, dads have a stronger influence. This is especially valid for women who choose nontraditional careers. At this point, the father seems to become more of a role model for his daughter, who comes to rely on his expertise and advice.[15]

Almquist and Angrist state well the uniqueness of those women who choose to pursue careers:

> The unconventional chooser is not so much a renegade as she is a product of additional enriching experiences which lead to a less stereotyped and broader conception of the female role. She does not reject the customary, time-honored duties of adult women, but sees them as augmented by work as an important feature of her adult life.[16]

Clearly, if more role models were available, more women would be encouraged to brave the wilds of the male-dominated organization. But until that time, probably the most likely spot for a woman to receive encouragement is from her parents, women faculty, or even male peers.

Mentors

But the best situation of all is to find a mentor. The mentor, a senior member of an organization, serves as a coach who teaches, advises and critiques a neophyte, preparing that beginner for more powerful positions and bringing her to the attention of the right people at the right time.

Writers of management books volley back and forth the issue of how vital it is for a woman to have a mentor. Most women find that, while it's possible to make it without one, the cost is much higher, and the process is much longer.

Of course, part of the reason for the debate on the necessity of mentors is that such helpers are rare for women. Because few women are available to serve as mentors (and some have a queen-bee attitude of keeping a regal distance from young women who have not paid the same high price for status), women tend to find mentors among men. And that, too, has its intrinsic difficulties in perceived and sometimes actual sexual interest.

While mystery seems to shroud how to acquire a mentor, most individuals who have such a sponsor did their work competently, were willing to take some risks to be noticed, and soon found themselves in a newly sprouted relationship with someone in the upper echelons. There's little one can do to land such a relationship, except to place oneself in a visible spot and respond quickly and positively when noticed. Of course, prayer would be a wise place to begin the search for a mentor.

Once you meet someone you'd like to imitate (somewhat), encourage that relationship. Let the other person know you want to excel in your present position and are open to advice and teaching as well as promotion. Make sure you *both* benefit from the experience. Sincerely care for your mentor as a person and not just as a means to achieve your own end. See to it that the relationship is reciprocal. And keep it free of any *sexual* entanglements—real or suggested.

I have acquired two mentors and have served as mentor for a few people. That was before I even knew such a term existed. Such a naive view is probably more possible in a Christian organization where caring for one's subordinates is emphasized more. We might call it discipling or shepherding, but it serves the same purpose as mentoring and generally carries with it a stronger emotional link between the two parties.

In nursing, too, obtaining a mentor is easier just because women are dominant in that profession. Carolyn, who is in a supervisory position, can quickly tick off what she's learned from her mentor: to maintain an open-door policy; to communicate inherent trust in the people who work for you; to inform your supervisor when you've made a mistake rather than try to cover up.

"She's the only director who gets into scrub clothes every day and makes rounds as a social event," Carolyn says about her mentor. "People can't say that she doesn't know what's going on." You can tell by the way Carolyn describes her that she wants to emulate her supervisor and not miss any valuable lessons she has to offer.

Left Adrift?

But if no mentor comes along to help a woman, all is not lost. She has alternatives. As one career consultant stated,

> A much more viable concept is for women at a peer level to act as mentor to each other as opposed to looking for that illusory butterfly, the mentor. . . . Most sharp gamesmen understand that you don't want one mentor anyway, because if the mentor falls into bad graces, usually the people on his coattails go with him. Therefore, it makes sense to have several sponsors in the company.[17]

Plus, the essential information that flows outside office channels can be gleaned in trade groups and professional societies rather than through the "old-boy network" that takes place on the golf course, in the locker room or at the bar.[18]

The point is that enough women have made it to the top to prove one thing: You don't have to be male or to find a mentor to slip into important slots on the organizational chart. While a mentor can boost you over the wall you're trying to scale, there are other ways to get over it. God is quite capable of using several means, not just one, of getting his will done.

Joseph's career (Genesis 37 and 39-41) displays some intriguing methods God can use to promote a person that *he* is backing. Joseph's first mentor was probably his father, who loved him with a special love because Joseph was born late in Jacob's life and because he was the beloved Rachel's first child. Joseph was placed in a favored position over his brothers, much to their chagrin.

They therefore removed him from the scene by selling him as a slave; thus he ended up in Egypt. His owner, Potiphar, became his next mentor. Potiphar saw that God was with Joseph. So Potiphar gave Joseph the position of general manager, which meant that he oversaw all Potiphar's property.

Joseph reciprocated Potiphar's care for him by refusing to give Potiphar's wife the sexual attention she demanded. Joseph pointed out that Potiphar had shared everything in the house but his wife with Joseph, and he intended to respect that generosity.

But Joseph was falsely accused and sent to jail. There, because of God's kindness, Joseph became the warden's assistant. Then, once again, it became apparent to a man in leadership that Joseph possessed outstanding qualities. Pharaoh appointed Joseph to the post of prime minister, where he diligently worked as Egypt's second in command.

Dramatic events cycled through Joseph's life. Yet in each situation, Joseph responded the same way: he saw God at work in circumstances; he worked hard and faithfully for his employer; and he displayed intense loyalty to his mentor.

These three principles can also keep a woman's path straight today as she strives to move consistently in her career. But, ultimately, it is God who blesses and provides advancement—sometimes by letting us be "sold into slavery" and "thrown into prison." He has his own ways of "mentoring" us and building necessary qualities within us.

But Who?

1. To help you espy someone you would like to be your mentor, make a list of the qualities *and* values you want in a mentor. Remember, this person will have a vast influence over you, and you will become his or her reflection in ways that you

might not at first imagine.

    2. If no mentor is on the horizon, consider:

    a. What peers can I learn from?

    b. What can each person teach me?

    c. What can I offer each of them?

    d. Who seems to have close connections with others in this organization or another? How can that person help me? How can I help that person?

    e. Are there natural gatherings (trade groups, professional societies) where I can find networks? If not, should I institute some group meetings to serve that purpose?

CHAPTER 13

Women Wielding Power

The setting is a hotel meeting room. The hotel's name is emblazoned across the podium, and the cushioned chairs are carefully color-coordinated with the room.

The career consultant conducting the business seminar for women asks, "How many of you would like to be more powerful?" Half to two-thirds of the women raise their hands.

The consultant isn't surprised; the reaction is typical. Yet he can't help but think about how men respond when he asks the same question. Every one of them raises his hand. Men want power.[1]

Most women, however, see power as negative. They view power as controlling, overbearing or even destroying people. It's power *for* oneself and power *over* others.[2]

But power does not have to be employed only to achieve
negative or self-centered results. Power is also the ability to get
things done, to mobilize resources, to influence.

Pushing Away Power

Women tend to shun power because they are inexperienced at
using it openly.[3] In this chapter, we will concentrate on what
power is and what it can accomplish positively. We will not
spend so much time on the abuse of power because that has
been covered in other writings in considerable detail. Besides,
abusive power is what women know best; they've often been its
victim.

Studies show that wielding power well is an important part
of being an effective leader. Power can be your most important
tool as far as your subordinates are concerned.

The classic study done in this area is by Donald Pelz.[4] He
documented what made subordinates satisfied. As he began the
study, he thought the factors would be the supervisors' abilities
to communicate, to be supportive and to recommend for promotion. But his research proved that the power the supervisor
had outside the group and upward in the organization was the
key factor. What concerned men and women was the impact
their supervisor made on overall policies and decisions. A nice
boss is nice, but that's not enough.[5]

What those workers were recognizing, even though they may
not have realized it, is that power begets power. The purpose
of this book is not to examine the ethics of such a system (that
would require a book in itself), but to recognize that business
functions this way. People who are viewed as having prestige
and status are much more likely to receive cooperation than
people who are viewed as having a lower status.[6]

People who look like they can command more of the organization's resources, who look like they can bring something
that is valued from outside into the group, who seem to have

access to the inner circles that make the decisions affecting the fate of individuals in organizations, may also be more effective as leaders of those around them—and be better liked in the process.[7]

Kanter asked twenty Indsco executives to define the effective manager's characteristics. The term they came up with as most important was *credibility,* which to them meant competence plus power. They also decided that credibility had to be directed upward in the organizational structure. If a person had influence upward, he or she also had it downward.[8]

Powerless People

People experiencing lack of upward influence respond in fairly predictable ways. Because of the restrictions they feel themselves, they in turn restrict others. People who are afraid they are powerless flex "power" muscles with their subordinates. Kanter explains that such a response isn't surprising:

If they have less call on the organizations' resources, less backup and support from sponsors and managers, less cooperative subordinates, and less influence in the informal power structure, people can only use the strongest tools at their disposal: disciplines or threats or maintaining tight control over all of the activities in their jurisdiction. . . . It is a vicious cycle: powerless authority figures who use coercive tactics provoke resistance and aggression, which prompts them to become more coercive, controlling, and behaviorally restrictive.[9]

One of the devices powerless people use is "the rules."[10] Because of "the rules" something must be done or not done a certain way. They employ a traditional line to answer every imaginable question: "It's policy."

Another response to powerlessness is to play it safe and assume a low-risk posture.[11] All the details of a project are surveyed with squinty eyes to make sure everything is perfect. Creativity may be lacking, the ideas stale and uninventive, but every detail is in place.

With the low-risk posture comes the need to jealously guard the domain. The person becomes very narrow in his or her interests and abilities and becomes "an expert," as do those reporting to that unit. The area is insulated, and the supervisor insists others come to him or her as an expert who approves their work.[12]

As one understands how power and the lack of it affects a supervisor, some of the clichés regarding women in leadership make sense: women lack clout; women don't delegate; women are too bossy. As one journalist noted,

[A woman's workers] fear she's less likely to be promoted, less likely to stick her neck out for them, get raises for them. They are reluctant to work for her because they feel their opportunities to move will be less. They say the odds are against her growing up to be president of their organization, so their chances will not be good.[13]

What "they say" is right. These workers have correctly tallied the score and found themselves losers because they work for a powerless supervisor.

One study specifically explored how a woman managed the external boundaries of her area of responsibility, how powerful she was upward and outward. The case study involved Dr. A, who was manager of a mental health center. Her troublesome areas lay in sustaining ties with the total organization and protecting the group from intrusion.[14]

Ties to other units were tenuous, and took the form of Dr. A's friendly but distant relationships with other Unit Chiefs and division heads, with little collaborative work. She accepted the fact of the organization's male dominance without question and saw herself as appropriately dealt with when she was being subtly derogated or isolated on the basis of gender. Finding it difficult to address the external boundary issues, Dr. A spent a large portion of her time with internal issues, particularly her staff's interpersonal relations. . . . Dr. A had difficulties in conceptualizing and carrying out the protective function.[15]

Clearly, this woman not only projected an ineffective image in attempting to protect her people but also was powerless to help them advance or to even present her unit in a winsome light to the rest of the organization.

Not only do powerless supervisors lack clout, but they also tend to be bossy. So the image of the bossy woman, unfortunately, has some truth to it. But any person who feels powerless may take a steely approach to leading.

One researcher in World War 2 observed people complaining about the bossiness of women supervisors who were inexperienced in their new roles. Yet he observed that newly promoted men given supervisory jobs without sufficient training showed the same tendencies as the women.[16] An insecure supervisor is an insecure supervisor whether that person is a he or a she. All weak people are the second sex.

But the sad reality is that a preference for men as managers is a preference for power. Past experience teaches that few women move far or well within an organization. Even if they do move, they usually can't take anyone with them.

The Hard Question

Before a woman decides to take a leadership role, she needs to pause long. It's one thing to say people have prejudged women and kept them from all they can be; it's quite another to say: "I don't care if people will achieve less in their careers because they end up reporting to me. I want the position, and I don't care what happens to anyone else."

If you decide to take the leadership role, you must also decide to be rigorous in your fight for your people and to cultivate power for your subordinates' sake as well as your own. They have been entrusted to your care, and you are expected to do everything you can to help them reach their full potential. Sometimes that means taking the risky path rather than the safe one you're longing to claim. That may mean choosing the welfare of that person over your own—even if advancement in your own career is the price tag. But those are important principles to decide on even before you accept a leadership role, for once in that position, it's tempting to respond as a powerless, shortsighted person or as a person who invests energy in gaining power for self—and only for self.

Before I became manager of a publications department, I made two ground rules that I refused to break: always to choose people over product, if a choice had to be made; and always to choose others over myself. I was not perfect in living those out; and I'm ashamed of the damage my inability may have caused in other peoples' lives.

But I think I managed for the most part to embrace those precepts in my daily decisions. That gave my subordinates a sense of my concern for their welfare. They also knew that if they were struggling in a relationship with a client I would back them up and take the pressure off them if it got too intense. I didn't know it then, but both those principles were foundational—though certainly not complete—in the maintenance of internal affairs and external boundaries.

Making an Impact

But admitting that power is necessary for effective leadership, how does one go about attaining power? Especially if one is a woman? Kanter states that three ingredients are inherent in every situation that increases one's power. First, one must find a task that is extraordinary and carry it out well. "Neither persons nor organizations get 'credit' for doing the mandatory or the expected," she states. A person might decide to be the first to take a new position, make organizational changes, or take a major risk and succeed.[17]

"The rewards go to innovators," Kanter writes, "not to the second one to do something; the first to volunteer for extra work exhibits 'leadership,' a quality anyone after that seems to lack."[18]

Visibility comprises another necessary ingredient in any power-building situation. Positions with special impact are those that straddle organizational units or cross the boundary between the organization and its environment.[19]

Finally, to gain power, one must complete a relevant activity. She will help solve a pressing organizational problem.[20]

Alliances can also serve as bridges to greater power. A mentor, for example, can help generate power because he or she is in a position to fight for you, to stand up for you in meetings, and to put you forth to receive promotions. A mentor also provides a means for you to express your need or concern, allowing you to be heard. And the mentor provides reflected power. The association with the mentor loans power to the young "water walker," as some organizations call workers backed by mentors.[21]

Peers also can help provide power. As one manager said, "To become powerful, people must first be successful and receive recognition, but they must wear the respect with a lack of arrogance. . . . They help their peers." They exchange information, and they bargain and trade with peers.[22]

Then there is the power that subordinates can imbue on a manager. Higher-level people need the loyalty and backing of their workers. They want a team behind them, and they work hard to pull one together. It's one thing to create a plan, but your team must be willing to carry it out every day.

An important quality of a powerful leader is the ability to know how to make subordinates feel powerful in their own right. Jane Evans, president of a company at age 25, said regarding her relationships with her staff, "I expect them to carry the ball by developing their own jobs without my constant supervision. They tell me I'm a great cheerleader."[23]

Dr. A was a woman who lacked power.[24] On several occasions, she delegated responsibility for certain tasks to others in the unit. They would complete the work differently than directed or would have someone else do the work. Dr. A was displeased, but she didn't directly confront them.

At times male subordinates even attempted to "seduce" Dr. A out of her role, thereby negating her authority over them. Once, in the middle of a conversation, a male paraprofessional began to compliment her on her style of dress and figure. Confused by the unexpected and inappropriate remark, she tried to return to her role without directly confronting his remark. She was powerless.

Leadership by Influence

When I'm in authority I like to keep in mind a picture of a strong leader, one I call an influence leader. This is the person who does not lead by virtue of an organizational chart or a salary figure but by the strength of her character. That is the kind of person I want to be. But I had trouble keeping that in mind on the first day I taught as an official faculty member at a seminary.

I entered the room feeling confident of myself and my material. I had taught this material in class as a guest lecturer the year before. It had been well received. I expected the same that day.

But instead I found myself being challenged every time I made a point. Hands were constantly raised with questions—some inane, some good. But I wasn't moving well through the material.

"Maybe," I thought, "I should just look at my notes rather than the students. If I don't recognize the questions, we'll at least cover all the material." I suspected I was being conspired against; certainly I wasn't being accorded the respect a faculty member receives even if *he's* inept.

But I just kept teaching and answering questions, pretending nothing was amiss. As I moved on I thought, "Tomorrow I'll bring in a male faculty member. That'll make this group behave." Then I realized my response was an escape, not a solution. I was like a baby sitter who can't handle the kids, so she calls in her boyfriend to glower at them. If I couldn't figure this out myself, I shouldn't be teaching. The tension—and panic—inside me mounted.

Finally, halfway through the class, I realized I had to make a choice: either take the stiff-arm approach and attempt to force my way to the end of the class time, or establish myself as someone who remains calm when under fire, someone who leads through strength of character. I wasn't at all sure the latter described me, but I wanted it to. I knew the tough-guy technique would fail miserably. Who was I to attempt to bulldoze my message into the minds of these students? They would respond to me as an emotional female who had lost her cool.

Just then a hand shot up in the air to question my latest point. I had been saying that a good writer always creates an outline. Ed asked, with an intense look on his face but with twinkling eyes, "Are we to assume the apostle Paul wrote from an outline?" I'd never felt one twinge of curiosity about how Paul wrote.

But I surprised myself with my answer. "Are we to assume you're putting yourself on the same level as Paul?"

Fortunately, the remark had just the right effect. It let Ed and the rest of the class know that I was aware they were harassing me. To the men apparently it signaled that I could take their harassment and join in the game instead of becoming its victim.

The questions stopped and the tone of the class went from challenging to accepting. I had established myself and convinced them to believe in me. I had led through influence rather than force. While God deserves the credit for the impression I created, I discovered the benefits of leading through strength.

No Contest

If a woman attempts to be tough with men, they will feel attacked as males, and they will *not* be dominated by her. It becomes a contest that she will not win. A woman must establish herself as someone to be respected, not as the person someone handed authority to in a frenzied moment.

My experience corresponds with the findings from various tests. Subordinates see two factors as important for a woman leader that are not significant for male leaders: (1) a lack of hostility in her leadership style; and (2) the presence in the subordinates of a positive attitude toward women as leaders. I had to avoid the former to achieve the latter.

The same studies find that peers perceive dominance in female leaders as less acceptable than in men.[25] Because of both the subordinates' views and the peers' perceptions, it becomes supremely important for a woman to cultivate an appropriate leadership style.

Fortunately, I've encountered few such threatening moments in my career. Usually humor and the use of a confident style have saved the day. A few times a hard-line stand was necessary. And at times it has been best to move on to other issues and not yet press to change prejudicial behavior.

Each circumstance is unique and must be dealt with as such, with the woman trusting in her personal judgment and asking herself: "Why is this person responding to me only as a woman? Why can't he or she see beyond that?" Sometimes women will find they have encouraged that view through giddiness, coquettishness or their own insecurity. Sometimes women are so busy looking for a lack of acceptance from men that it is all they can see.

Overall, the best approach is for the woman to make sure she is convinced that she belongs in the position she's holding and that she doesn't need to apologize for having her job. If she believes in herself, others will tend to believe in her.

Not Flaunting Freedom
But she should be careful not to flaunt her freedom. If she encounters someone who is concerned about her place in the organization, it is important to recognize that the person probably has a narrow view of what a woman can do based on past and present female models. But more important, that individual may possess a limited perspective of his or her own personhood. It would be inappropriate and unkind to deal with an insecure person by attempting to verbally lambast him or her. Instead, deal with that person patiently and with respect. Try to hear the person's insecurity rather than his or her hurting words. Help to make him or her feel important.

Ginger employed that method with a fellow church staff member and two years later they were good friends who worked together well. Considering that they started out with him refusing to give her a room in which to conduct her class, her patience paid off with big dividends. She let him watch her lead. He eventually figured out that she was good at her job.

In another instance, Sandy discovered the importance of exploring why one man was put off by woman leaders. She was at Boston University, attending a conference to help Christian women define themselves in society outside the home. She met Mike at lunch. He was attending another conference at the university.

When Mike learned why she was there, he spent twenty minutes describing women's lack of involvement in early church history—no representative at the Nicene Council, the Jerusalem Council, and so on.

Sandy laid down her fork and offered this response: "I can't answer you point for point. But I'm not sure it would make any difference. I sense a lot of pain underneath your statements. Is that true?" Mike bowed his head and tears started to flow. He told her of his crumbling marriage and the despair and pain he felt. Sandy had employed confidence, gentleness and caring. And the "woman's issue" turned out not to be the issue.

Of course, not every encounter will have such a happy ending. Phyllis got up before a group to speak, and the men threw paper wads at her. Jane was denied the chance to counsel people because other church staff members felt it was inappropriate for a woman to do so, even though Jane had more experience than any of the men and was willing to limit herself to counseling women. Some people who place limits on women may never respond well to women in leadership.

There comes a time when you need to accept that troublesome person in your life as having a narrow scope and move on to other matters rather than letting it absorb your emotional energy. God is still in the business of protecting and caring for his own, and no person can thwart his intent for you. Jane, who wasn't allowed to counsel in her church, found several needy neighbors. Soon they were attending her church, becoming Christians, and showing up at the church office to have Jane help them with their problems. Now she is accepted as counselor by the other church staff, who laugh about how Jane got the position by going through the back door. Jane will tell you that God created the door.

But the important point when encountering the immovable ones is not to harbor resentments toward them but to remember that 1 Peter 4:19 applies to your life: Entrust yourself to your faithful Creator and continue to do what is right. And be gentle.

Steps to Follow
One of the toughest situations for a woman manager is dealing

with a male subordinate. Here are some specific pointers that can help.[26]

1. Realize you don't have to play the power game in every encounter. Don't stay seated behind your desk all the time. Come out from behind the desk or go to his office.

2. Don't reprimand him in public. Tell him your concerns privately. Be firm.

3. Anticipate uncomfortable situations. For example, don't let him give a presentation that is so bad you have to step in to rescue him. Preview the presentation.

4. Don't be defensive about being a manager. If he acts in an unproductive manner, call him in and ask him why he does it that way. If his language is offensive, don't take it personally but inform him that such behavior will not be rewarded.

5. Don't compete with him. Don't let anything become an issue of his manhood versus your womanhood. Hit problems directly. Treat them as managerial problems, performance problems, money problems. Don't let them be a woman's problem.

6. Use naiveté to handle situations fraught with sexual suggestions. Don't hear remarks that are suggestive, or don't catch the double meaning of a statement. Change the subject.

7. Watch out for flattery. Sometimes you may find yourself flattered by a remark and flirt back. Or you blush and look dismayed. The man's ego becomes involved at this point. Before he was just playing and testing. He recognized that he might win and he might lose. But if his ego becomes involved either through your encouragement or your confusion, he may threaten you. The situation gets complicated if he's your supervisor or in a senior position. At this point, test his threat. Let him know you don't intend to be coerced.

Just in case he gets insistent, keep a log of each conversation—what was said, where, when, and under what circumstances. Write a report and have it placed in your personnel file. Record all the details. Request a job transfer and follow up on it. Meantime, keep your distance.

If the situation becomes extreme, you can sue. Legal precedent has been set and laws have been written to protect you. This is where detailed personal records are important. Keep your record not only of the exchanges with the man but also whom you told, when, and which details.

Above all, recognize that you do not have to give in to sexual pressure or lose your job. You can take action.

Many women don't expect to be the object of sexual harassment. But it may be more common than they realize. *Redbook* conducted a survey in which they found that nine out of ten working women experienced some form of sexual harassment on the job.[27] So be prepared not to hear or see or understand. It can keep you out of all sorts of problems and enable you to respond with a subtle expression of personal power.

Can Power Be Feminine?

Just how do women's qualities dovetail with all this talk about power? A woman's tendency to be vulnerable, giving, flexible, cooperative and closely tied to others might seem to keep power at bay.

But these characteristics themselves don't thwart power. Instead, influence fails when women express these characteristics in weak, negative ways. Vulnerability becomes tuning into others' emotions and not your own. Giving becomes a method to gain acceptance. Flexibility gets expressed only at home. Cooperation becomes a way to avoid risk. And closeness binds us into an unsatisfying search for someone to make us happy. Each bent expression comes down to limiting views of oneself and to attitudes of subservience, lack of dignity and lack of freedom. These are the opposite of power.

But these qualities are beautiful when expressed as strengths for then they can lead to a positive use of power for yourself and for those in your life. That brings us back to where we started in this book. We have looked at all sorts of questions together:

Career vs. home—do you have to choose?

Career vs. job—why choose one or the other?

Being a token—how will you respond?

Success—what is it to you?

Masculinity vs. femininity—what does it mean to be womanly?

Strengths vs. weaknesses—how do you mend your broken femininity?

Role models—do you need them?

Power—how do you use it?

All of these add up to the biggest question of all: Can you be a womanly leader?

The confusion one feels in searching for answers can leave one in turbulence. Like a rough sea, it's enough to drown even a proficient swimmer. As I paddle my way over—and under—the waves, I remember the life preservers I have: God, my friends, my love of challenges, the sense of what I ought to be, and the sense of what I can be. In his poem "Adam's Curse," William Butler Yeats's "beautiful woman" says, "To be born woman is to know—although they do not talk of it at school—that we must labor to be beautiful."[28]

Learning how to be a giving and receiving whole woman who knows how to express womanly qualities in various settings is a task to last a lifetime. But to be beautiful, one must choose to work at it.

Notes

Chapter 1: The Door of Opportunity

[1]Karen Burton Mains, "It's a Mystery to Me: Struggles with Sexual Ambiguity in the Church," *Christianity Today,* 17 July 1981, p. 56.

[2]"Women Executives: What Holds Us Back?" *U.S. News & World Report,* 8 February 1982, p. 64.

[3]Bob Phillips, *A Time to Laugh* (Irvine, Calif.: Harvest House, 1977), pp. 20-21.

[4]Philip Goldberg, "Are Women Prejudiced Against Women?" *Transaction* 5 (1968): 28-30.

[5]Virginia Ellen Schein, "Sex Roles Stereotypes and Requisite Management Characteristics," *Journal of Applied Psychology,* June 1975, p. 342.

Chapter 2: Inner Conflicts

[1]Edwin C. Lewis, *Developing Woman's Potential* (Ames, Iowa: Iowa State Univ. Press, 1968), p. 157.

[2]Anne Steinmann and David J. Fox, "Male-Female Perceptions of the Female Role in the United States," *Journal of Psychology* 64 (1966): 265-76.

[3]Lewis, *Developing Woman's Potential,* p. 292.

[4]Margaret Hennig and Anne Jardim, *The Managerial Woman* (New York: Simon and Schuster, 1976), p. 59.

[5]Ibid.

[6]Ibid.

Chapter 3: The Only Woman

[1]Rosabeth Moss Kanter, *Men and Women of the Corporation* (New York: Basic Books, 1977). For a brief and visual presentation, see Rosabeth Moss Kanter

with Barry A. Stein, *A Tale of "O": On Being Different in an Organization* (New York: Harper & Row, 1980).

[2]Kanter, *Men and Women,* p. 212.

[3]Ibid., p. 214.

[4]Ibid., p. 213.

[5]Ibid., p. 231.

[6]Ibid., p. 232.

[7]Ibid., p. 233.

[8]Marilyn Bendu, "When the Boss Is a Woman," *Esquire,* 28 March 1978, p. 36.

[9]Kanter, *Men and Women,* p. 230.

[10]Margaret Mead, *Male and Female: A Study of the Sexes in a Changing World* (New York: William Morrow, 1949), p. 377.

Chapter 4: Do We Fear Success?

[1]Matina Horner, "Fail: Bright Women," *Psychology Today,* June 1969, p. 36.

[2]L. A. Peplau, "Impact of fear of success and sex-role attitudes on women's competitive achievement," *Journal of Personality and Social Psychology* 34, no. 4 (1976): 561-68.

[3]L. Monahan, D. Kuhn and P. Shaver, "Intra-psychic vs. cultural explanations of the 'Fear of Success' motive," *Journal of Personality and Social Psychology* 29 (January 1974): 60-64.

[4]Kanter, *Men and Women,* p. 221.

[5]Ibid., pp. 140, 160-61.

[6]Ibid.

[7]Ibid., pp. 151-52.

[8]"For Lots of Working Women, 'Price of Success Is Too High,' " *U.S. News & World Report,* December 1981, p. 76.

[9]Jane Adams, "Conversations with Successful Men," *Working Woman,* November 1981, pp. 92-94.

[10]Ibid.

[11]Malcolm Ritter, "Family plus career needn't strain women mentally, say studies," *The Grand Rapids Press,* 12 September 1984, D-7.

[12]Esther Matthews, *Counseling Girls and Women Over the Life Span* (Falls Church, Va.: American Personnel and Guidance Assoc., 1972), pp. 31-32.

[13]Ibid.

[14]Ibid.

[15]Lewis, *Developing Woman's Potential,* p. 75.

[16]Jane Adams, *Women on Top* (New York: Hawthorne Books, 1979), p. 206.

[17]"Price Too High," p. 76.

[18]Hennig and Jardim, *Managerial Woman,* p. 37.

[19]Ibid., p. 38.

[20]Ibid., p. 39.

[21]Dorothy Sayers, *Are Women Human?* (Downers Grove, Ill.: InterVarsity Press, 1971), p. 24.

[22]Quoted in Paul Tournier, *The Gift of Feeling* (Atlanta: John Knox Press, 1979), p. 20.

[23]Ibid., p. 21.

[24]Sayers, *Are Women Human?* pp. 24-25.

Chapter 5: Male and Female Differences

[1]Mary Anne Warren, "Androgyny," *The Nature of Woman: An Encyclopedia and Guide to the Literature* (Inverness, Calif.: Edgepress, 1980), p. 16.

[2]John Lee, "The Eleventh Megatrend," *Time,* 23 July 1984, p. 104.

[3]Janet Shibley Hyde and B. G. Rosenberg, *Half the Human Experience* (Lexington, Mass.: D. C. Health, 1980), p. 59.

[4]Jan Morris and Annie Leibovitz, "Gender Games," *Vanity Fair,* June 1984, pp. 44-47.

[5]Pamela Weintraub, "The Brain: His and Hers," *Discover,* April 1981, pp. 15-20.

[6]Ibid., pp. 19-20.

[7]Ibid., p. 17.

[8]Ibid., p. 18.

[9]David Gelman et al., "Just How the Sexes Differ," *Newsweek,* 18 May 1981, pp. 78, 81.

[10]Ibid., p. 73.

[11]Eman F. Hammer, "Creativity and feminine ingredients in young male artists," *Perceptual and Motor Skills* 19 (1964): 414.

[12]Lewis, *Developing Woman's Potential,* p. 69.

[13]Anne Ulanov, *Receiving Woman: Studies in the Psychology and Theology of the Feminine* (Philadelphia: Westminster Press, 1981), p. 166.

[14]Mead, *Male and Female,* pp. 371-72.

[15]Ibid.

[16]M. Esther Harding, *The Way of All Women* (New York: Putnam, 1970), pp. 71-72.

[17]Ibid.

[18]Ibid., p. 75.

[19]Ibid., p. 76.

[20]Hennig and Jardim, *Managerial Woman,* pp. 154-81.

[21]Ibid., pp. 166-67.

[22]Ibid., pp. 172-73.

[23]Ibid., p. 179.

[24]Alma Baron, "Do Managers Clone Themselves?" *Working Woman,* September 1981, p. 100.

[25](Ann Arbor: Servant Pub., 1980), pp. 13-14.

[26]Mead, *Male and Female,* pp. 383-84.

Chapter 6: A Woman's Strengths

[1]Patricia Ward and Martha Stout, *Christian Women at Work* (Grand Rapids, Mich.: Zondervan, 1981), p. 40.

[2]W. E. Vine, *An Expository Dictionary of Old Testament Words* (Old Tappan, N.J.: Fleming Revell, 1978), p. 81.

[3]Ward and Stout, *Christian Women,* pp. 89-90.

[4]Janet Giele, *Women and the Future* (New York: Free Press, 1978), p. 34.

[5]Veronica F. Nieva and Barbara A. Gutek, *Women and Work: A Psychological Perspective* (New York: Praeger Pub., 1981), p. 60.

[6]Ulanov, *Receiving Woman,* p. 15.

[7]Patricia Nancy Feulner, *Women in the Professions: A Social-Psychological Study* (Palo Alto, Calif.: R & E Research Associates, 1979), pp. 33-58.

[8]Natalie Shainess, "Is anatomy destiny? Panel: The changing role of women psychiatrists," *Journal of American Medical Workers Association* 28 (1973): 295.

[9]Ibid.

[10]Ibid.

[11]Adams, *Women on Top,* p. 29.

[12]Bendu, "When the Boss," p. 41.

[13]John G. Geier, "Personal Profile System" (Performax Systems International, 1977), p. 5.

[14]Warren Bennis, "Sex Roles and the Business World," *San Jose Mercury News,* 22 March 1981.

[15]Ibid.

[16]Ibid.

[17]Ibid.

Chapter 7: Open Communication

[1]Hyde and Rosenberg, *Half the Human Experience,* pp. 158-59.

[2]John Baird, Jr., "Sex Differences in Group Communication: A Review of Relevant Research," *Quarterly Journal of Speech,* April 1976, pp. 181-84.

[3]Jean Baker Miller, *Toward a New Psychology of Women* (Boston: Beacon Press, 1976), p. 30.

[4]Ulanov, *Receiving Woman,* p. 164.

Chapter 8: A Giving Spirit

[1]Miller, *Toward a New Psychology,* p. 49.

[2]Ibid.

[3]Ibid.

[4]Rae Carlson, "Sex differences in ego functioning: Exploratory studies of agency and communication," *Journal of Consulting and Clinical Psychology* 37, no. 2 (1971): 267-77.

[5]Gladys Hunt, "A New Look at Christian Wives," paper presented at the Continental Congress on the Family, St. Louis, Missouri, October 1975, pp.

6-7.
[6]Ibid.
[7]Miller, *Toward a New Psychology*, p. 50.

Chapter 9: Flexibility for New Challenges
[1]Hyde and Rosenberg, *Half the Human Experience*, p. 100.
[2]Miller, *Toward a New Psychology*, p. 54.
[3]Hyde and Rosenberg, *Half the Human Experience*, p. 101.
[4]Miller, *Toward a New Psychology*, p. 44.
[5]Ibid.
[6]Ibid.
[7]Ibid., p. 55.
[8]Ibid.
[9]Ibid., p. 56.
[10]Ibid.
[11]Adams, *Women on Top*, p. 21.
[12]Ibid., p. 23.
[13]Ibid., p. 25.
[14]Ibid.
[15]Ibid., p. 22.

Chapter 10: A Cooperative Nature
[1]John Baird, "Sex Differences in Group Communication," pp. 188-89.
[2]Adams, *Women on Top*, p. 102.
[3]Ibid., p. 103.
[4]Miller, *Toward a New Psychology*, p. 53.
[5]G. R. Mintz, "Some observations on the function of women sociologists at sociology conventions," *American Sociologist*, August 1967, pp. 158-59.
[6]Hennig and Jardim, *Managerial Woman*, p. 47.
[7]Ibid.
[8]Jeanne Block, "Issue, Problems, and Pitfalls in Assessing Sex Differences: A Critical Review of the Psychology of Sex Differences," *Merrill-Palmer Quarterly* 22 (1976): 283-308.

Chapter 11: Close Connections
[1]Miller, *Toward a New Psychology*, p. 40.
[2]Harding, *Way of All Women*, p. 87.
[3]Miller, *Toward a New Psychology*, p. 83.
[4]Naida West, "Leadership and gender: A comparative analysis of male and female leadership in business, politics, and government," *Dissertation Abstracts International* 40 (March 1980): 5219A-5220A.
[5]Dorothy Haccoun, Robert Haccoun and George Sallay, "Sex differences in the appropriateness of supervisory styles: A nonmanagement view," *Journal*

of Applied Psychology 63 (February 1978): 124-26.

[6]Lewis, *Developing Woman's Potential*, p. 76.

[7]Ibid., p. 67.

[8]Hyde and Rosenberg, *Half the Human Experience*, p. 85.

[9]Miller, *Toward a New Psychology*, p. 85.

[10]Ibid.

[11]Lewis, *Developing Woman's Potential*, p. 76.

[12]Miller, *Toward a New Psychology*, p. 91.

[13]Ibid.

[14]Ibid., p. 93.

[15]Ibid.

[16]Adams, *Women on Top*, pp. 12-17.

[17]Ibid., p. 17.

[18]Ibid., p. 14.

[19]Ibid.

[20]Ibid., p. 15.

[21]Miller, *Toward a New Psychology*, p. 129.

[22]Ibid.

[23]Ibid.

[24]Ibid., p. 93.

[25]Ibid., p. 131.

[26]William J. Kreidler, "How Well Do You Resolve Conflict?" *Instructor*, January 1984, pp. 30-33.

Chapter 12: Finding a Role Model

[1]Adams, *Women on Top*, p. 28.

[2]"When Women Take Over as Bosses," *U.S. News & World Report*, 22 March 1982, p. 77.

[3]U.S. Department of Labor Bureau of Statistics, August 1985.

[4]Giele, *Women and the Future*, p. 12.

[5]Ward and Stout, *Christian Women*, p. 187.

[6]Elizabeth A. Ashburn, *Motivation, Personality and Work-Related Characteristics of Women in Male-Dominated Professions* (Washington, D.C.: National Association for Women Deans, Administrators and Counselors, 1977), p. 12.

[7]Nieva and Gutek, *Women and Work*, p. 59.

[8]Kanter, *Men and Women*, p. 58.

[9]Hennig and Jardim, *Managerial Woman*, p. 13.

[10]Mead, *Male and Female*, pp. 374-75.

[11]Elizabeth M. Almquist and Shirley S. Angrist, "Role Model Influence on College Women's Career Aspirations," *Merrill-Palmer Quarterly* 17 (1971): 263-379.

[12]Ashburn, *Motivation, Personality*, pp. 8-9.

[13]Ibid., p. 13.

[14]Ibid.
[15]Almquist and Angrist, "Role Model Influence," p. 264.
[16]Ibid.
[17]"Women Executives," p. 64.
[18]Ibid.

Chapter 13: Women Wielding Power
[1]"Women Executives," p. 63.
[2]Miller, *Toward a New Psychology*, p. 116.
[3]Ibid.
[4]Donald Pelz, "Influence: A Key to Effective Leadership in the First-Line Supervisor," *Personnel* 29 (1952): 3-11.
[5]Ibid.
[6]Kanter, *Men and Women*, p. 168.
[7]Ibid., p. 169.
[8]Ibid.
[9]Ibid., p. 190.
[10]Ibid., p. 192.
[11]Ibid.
[12]Ibid.
[13]Bendu, "When the Boss," p. 41.
[14]Marjorie Bayes and Peter M. Newton, "Women in Authority: A sociopsychological analysis," *Journal of Applied Behavioral Science* 14, no. 1 (1978): 11.
[15]Ibid., p. 12.
[16]Kanter, *Men and Women*, p. 205.
[17]Ibid.
[18]Ibid., p. 177.
[19]Ibid., p. 179.
[20]Ibid., p. 180.
[21]Ibid.
[22]Ibid., pp. 181-82.
[23]Ibid., p. 303.
[24]Bayes and Newton, "Women in Authority," pp. 14-15.
[25]Gertrude Heller, "A comparative study of women and men in organizational leadership roles," *Dissertation Abstracts International* 39 (June 1979): 6197-98.
[26]Bendu, "When the Boss," p. 41.
[27]"How Do You Handle Sex on the Job?" *Redbook*, January 1976, p. 74.
[28]William Butler Yeats, *The Norton Anthology of English Literature*, vol. 2 (New York: W. W. Norton, 1962), p. 1347.